BALANCING ACT

BALANCING ACT

Cutting Energy Subsidies While Protecting Affordability

Caterina Ruggeri Laderchi
Anne Olivier
Chris Trimble

THE WORLD BANK

Contents

Figures

Tables

Acknowledgments

This report is part of the Regional Study Program of the Europe and Central Asia Region of the World Bank, conducted under the leadership of the Regional Chief Economist, Indermit Gill.

The report has been prepared by a team in the regional poverty group (Poverty Reduction and Economic Management Sector Unit), working under the guidance of Indermit Gill, Chief Economist ECA Region, Yvonne Tsikata, Sector Director, Poverty Reduction and Economic Management Sector Unit, and Benu Bidani, Sector Manager ECSP3. The team was composed of Caterina Ruggeri Laderchi (Team Leader), Anne Olivier, and Chris Trimble. Maria Shkaratan worked extensively in constructing and standardizing the data. Victoria Strokova and Ramya Sundaram of the Social Protection group made substantive contributions to chapter 5. Sofia Chiarucci and Michael Stanton-Geddes provided invaluable and timely research assistance. Maria Koreniako helped draft some of the boxes. Shane Streifel prepared a background note on energy pricing. Lena Makarenko and Akua Nkrumah provided support. Robert Zimmermann edited the report and Maureen Itepu and Maria Koreniako formatted it. Romain Falloux of El Vikingo Design, Inc. beautifully designed it.

While keeping full responsibility for any error or inaccuracies in this report, the team would like to thank a number of colleagues who have contributed in various capacities. The Peer Reviewers for this study, who contributed comments at various stages of report preparation, were Vivien Foster, Samuel Freje-Rodriguez, Ruslan Yemtsov, and Lucian Pop. As this report makes use of the data of the ECAPOV database, we are greatly indebted to Victor Sulla and Manami Suga for facilitating access to the data and the standardized welfare aggregate and for providing guidance on the use of the data, particularly in the delicate phase of standardizing energy variables across the different household surveys.

Given the multisectoral nature of this report, the team benefited from comments, wisdom, and bibliography provided by an extended group of colleagues from the ECA poverty cluster, the ECA Chief Economist Office, the ECA Energy Group, the ECA Social Protection group, and the Human Development Network Anchor. We would like to thank, in particular, Sandu Cojocaru of the ECA poverty cluster, Uwe Deichman and Fan Zhang of the ECA Chief Economist Office, Salvador Rivera, Yadviga Semikolenova, Gary Stuggins, and Claudia Vasquez Suarez from the ECA Energy group, Kathy Lindert, Ramya Sundaram, and Viktoria Strokova of the ECA HD group, and Ruslan Yemtsov and Lucian Pop from the Human Development Network Anchor. A number of other colleagues, including Rajna Cemerska, Plamen Danchev, Aleksan Hovhannisyan, Nino Moroshkina, Katerina Petrina, Peter Pojarski, Sashka Posarak, Julia Smolyar, and Owen Smith, helped us gather materials on specific programs referred to in the text or boxes.

In addition to the work of this regional overview, five case studies are being undertaken, three of which thanks to the generous support of the PSIA Trust Fund. The choice of countries aimed to reconcile the demands of the country programs and the need to reflect different stages in the transition to cost recovery in the energy sector. Work is almost completed on the Albania, Romania, and Serbia case studies and is starting on the Armenia and Tajikistan case studies. Preliminary insights of these case studies are reflected, as appropriate, in the text. The team would like to thank the colleagues with whom we are collaborating on these case studies: Sandu Cojocaru, Joost de Laat, Boryana Gotcheva, Vlad Grigoras, Melis Guven, Aylin Isik-Dikmelik, Sunil Khosla, Lorena Kostallari, Gregory Kisunko, Arthur Kochnakyan, Menahem Prywes, Salvador Rivera, Ramya Sundaram, Emil Tesliuc, and Salman Zaidi. A special thanks goes to Carrie Turk for designing and supervising qualitative work on energy consumption and use and for interest in various measures of supporting energy affordability. The insights provided by her work have greatly enriched our understanding and our policy dialogue to date.

A number of useful comments on both substance and presentation have been provided by participants at a number of events that have accompanied the preparation of this regional overview, including an HD Cappuccino seminar and at an internal seminar for the Chief Economist Office in the spring of 2011, the PSIA forum in November 2011, the ECA PREM learning event, the PSIA learning event, the Inequality and Public Policy Practice seminars held in the spring of 2012, all in Washington, DC, and at the Social Forum of the Energy Community held in Chisinau in October 2011.

Finally, we would like to thank the ECA Chief Economist, Indermit Gill, and William Van Eeghen, who manages the regional studies program in the Chief Economist Office, for the support and guidance that they have given us.

Abbreviations

CIS	Commonwealth of Independent States
CPCs	Candidate and Potential Candidate countries (EU)
EBRD	European Bank for Reconstruction and Development
EC	Energy Community
ECAPOV	Database of household survey for Eastern Europe and Central Asia
EPOC	Eastern Partnership and Other Commonwealth of Independent States countries
ESA	Energy-related social assistance
EU	European Union
EU MS	European Union Member State
GDP	gross domestic product
HBS	Household Budget Survey
LPG	liquefied petroleum gas
LRSA	Last Resort Social Assistance
LSMS	Living Standards Measurement Study

Overview

Introduction

The cost of energy in Eastern Europe and Central Asia, as elsewhere, is an important policy issue, as shown by the concerns for energy affordability during the past harsh winter.[1] Governments try to moderate the burden of energy expenditures that is experienced by households through subsidies to the energy providers, so that households pay tariffs below the cost recovery level for the energy they use. These subsidies result in significant pressures on government budgets when international prices rise. They also provide perverse incentives for the overconsumption of energy as households do not pay the true cost of energy, and therefore, have fewer incentives to save or to invest in energy efficiency.

Balancing competing claims—fiscal and environmental concerns which would push for raising energy tariffs on the one hand, and affordability and political economy concerns which push for keeping tariffs artificially low on the other—is a task that policy makers in the region are increasingly unable to put off. Addressing this issue is all the more pressing as the ongoing crisis continues to add stress to government budgets, and that international energy prices remain high. While challenging, the reforms needed for this balancing act can build on much that has been learned in the last decade about improving the effectiveness of social assistance systems and increasing energy efficiency. And the payoffs for these reforms could be substantial: we estimate that most countries in the region could save 0.5 to 1 percent of gross domestic product (GDP) by implementing the reforms.

This is the first report to assess, at the microlevel for the whole region, the distributional impact of raising energy tariffs to cost recovery levels and to simulate policy options to cushion these impacts. The analysis relies on a unique database of standardized household surveys that covers the majority of countries in the region (the ECAPOV database). This type of cross-country exercise requires a trade-off between the details of specific country situations with the benefits of a broad overview. While a set of separate case studies delves into the specific challenges different countries face, this report adopts broad country groupings to identify commonalities across subregions. These groups are named with respect to their position vis-à-vis the European Union (EU) and are EU member states (EU MSs), including the EU MSs of Central and Eastern Europe;[2] EU candidate and potential candidate countries (CPCs), including Croatia, Turkey, and the western Balkans; and the Eastern Partnership and Other Commonwealth of Independent States countries (EPOCs), which include the members of the Commonwealth of Independent States (CIS) and Georgia.

Before we proceed, it is worth noting that this report focuses on two main sources of energy used by households: electricity and gas. These account, respectively, for 4.5 and 1.6 percent of household spending, even though there is large variation across countries.[3] In addition to these sources, in some countries, households rely significantly on other sources such as district heating and hot water (most common in Latvia and Lithuania), coal (Kyrgyz Republic), and wood (Tajikistan). Of these, district heating is the source that, like electricity and gas, would be most affected by the international price of gas.[4,5]

Energy Affordability in a Broader Context

The experience of the past decade—a decade which saw energy price increases everywhere in Eastern Europe and Central Asia, even if with significant variation across countries—gives reasons for both concern and hope. Tariff adjustments are clearly possible, but, if not accompanied by improvements in efficiency, they are likely to be painful.[6] As figure 1 illustrates, higher prices for electricity (the most important energy source for households) are associated with higher burdens of electricity spending in household budgets. Households therefore appear to have limited ways of keeping their energy expenditures in check. Indeed, country evidence over time shows that energy price increases often result in households coping by cutting down on other types of basic consumption such as food or health spending. Despite concerns about energy affordability among households if higher tariffs are introduced, the last decade also shows that relatively rapid increases in energy efficiency are possible, and that those help households adapt to the higher prices environment. This is illustrated by the case of the EU MSs. This group of countries which today has

FIGURE 1
Electricity Price and Electricity Share of Total Household Expenditures

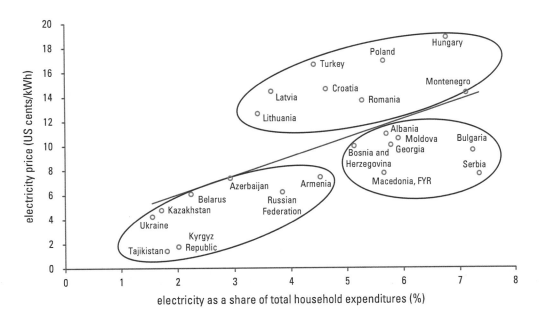

Sources: ECAPOV, World Bank estimates.

above average energy prices (note that in figure 1 they are mostly located above the line that describes the average relation between the share of spending on energy and energy prices) in 2000 had energy tariffs comparable with those in the countries of the CIS (around 5 U.S. cents/kWh, see chapter 1, figures 2.1-2.3). The significant increase in tariffs that EU MSs experienced over the decade has been accompanied and made possible by increases in efficiency which today result in the lowest physical consumption of electricity and gas per unit of output in the region.

To capture the plurality of factors that affect energy tariffs and their affordability for households, this report adopts a simple framework, which is illustrated in figure 2. The framework distinguishes the factors determining the technical cost of energy from those that affect energy affordability for households. Affordability (or its converse, vulnerability to tariff increases) depends on the way technical costs are translated into tariffs, how sectoral policies shape demand patterns, and the social protection measures available to support energy affordability. The balancing act governments are called to perform now requires a mix of subsidy reduction and investment in both sectoral policies and social protection to help households adapt to a new high tariff environment and to cushion the adverse distributional impact. For simplicity, in the framework, we identify predetermined elements reflecting country endowments or past

FIGURE 2
Framework

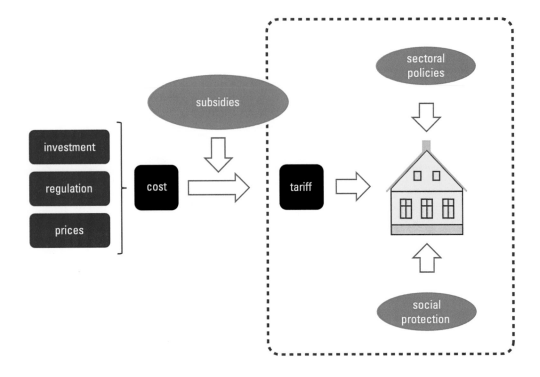

policies in blue that determine the current technical cost and current policy variables in green. These different elements are discussed below in turn, highlighting differences across regional subgroupings or countries.

The determinants of the technical costs of energy

The factors determining the cost of energy in any given country are numerous and complex, but, for the sake of simplicity, we may summarize them under three broad headings: prices, regulations, and investments. Note that, while these factors can be considered predetermined at any given time, they do change over time, particularly because of the influence of sectoral energy policies (for example, investment in alternative energy can change a country's dependence on existing energy sources and, therefore, its vulnerability to international prices and so on).

Prices refer to both the level of international prices and a country's vulnerability to them. Over the last decade, international prices have increased significantly and so has their variability as energy markets have undergone significant changes. Most relevant for Eastern Europe and Central Asia has been the tightening of global oil markets since the early

2000s because of strong global demand, the move of the Russian Federation to price gas more closely to market prices within bilateral monopoly arrangements, and the increase in competition in gas markets because of more tanker shipments of liquefied natural gas. Other global developments—such as the boom in new technologies that allow for horizontal drilling or the exploitation of shale gas—have not materialized directly in the region yet.

The extent to which countries have been affected by these developments and will be affected by future increases depends on the following:

i.   The extent of their reliance on imports: only five countries in the region do not rely on imports for their energy needs (starting from the largest exporter: Turkmenistan, Kazakhstan, Azerbaijan, Russia and Uzbekistan), while a half-dozen countries rely on imports for more than 90 percent of their total energy consumption (in order from most dependent: Moldova, Belarus, Slovakia, Armenia, Turkey, and Lithuania).

ii. The diversification of energy resources available to them: countries that are more diversified in terms of their energy resources are likely to be less exposed to international price changes. The 11 countries that obtain more than 50 percent of their fuel mix from one source are therefore more vulnerable to international prices.[7]

iii. Their energy intensity: countries that use energy more efficiently, all else constant, will be less exposed to the dynamics of international markets. Since the beginning of the transition, there have been significant improvements in energy efficiency across the region, which have been brought about by the shift from heavy to light industry and commercial services. But, as shown in figure 3, EPOC countries, in particular, still have the highest levels of energy intensity.[8]

Regulations in our framework refer to the broad set of regulations that govern the energy sector and tariff setting, in particular. The last decade has witnessed significant changes, particularly among EU MSs. Through the accession process, these countries have introduced comprehensive reform packages, including the unbundling of production and transmission, the strengthening of regulators, enhancing transparency in network operations, establishing wholesale and retail markets, and addressing tariff reform and affordability. figure 4 synthesizes the progress made by countries in the region according to the European Bank for Reconstruction and Development's (EBRD) index of infrastructure reform in the electricity sector. CPCs that are proceeding along the same path are likely to see similarly significant changes in the future, while some of the EPOC countries (Moldova, Ukraine) are also implementing this type of reforms

FIGURE 3
Energy Intensity, or Energy Use per US$1,000 GDP, 2008

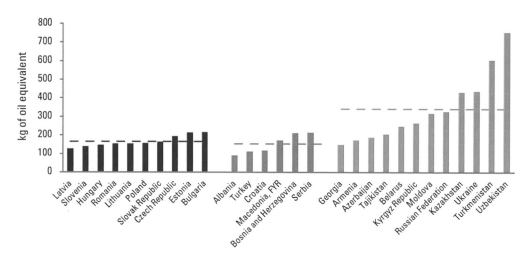

Source: World Development Indicators (database), World Bank, Washington, DC, http://data.worldbank.org/data-catalog/world-development-indicators.
Note: The figures shows results in constant 2005 purchasing power parity U.S. dollars.

FIGURE 4
EBRD Index of Infrastructure Reform in the Electricity Sector, 2000 and 2010

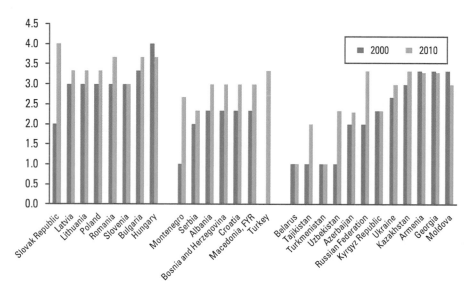

Sources: ECAPOV, World Bank estimates.
Note: Index ranges from 1 to 5, where 5 indicates maximum compliance with core best practices.

through their association or membership in the Energy Community (EC). An important set of regulations that will have a large impact on tariff setting in EU MSs (and, down the line, also the CPCs) is represented by the norms aimed at internalizing the social costs of energy production, which are related to both health costs and climate-related impacts.

The third set of factors determining the cost of energy in a given country is investments. This refers to both past investments, that determine the technology available to produce electricity or access different sources of energy (the presence of a gas pipeline), and future investments, particularly those needed to upgrade the capital base of the sector and allow it to face future demand. Recent estimates suggest that, for the region as a whole, these costs might amount to as much as US$3.3 trillion if a lights-out scenario is to be averted (World Bank 2010). Investment needs are going to be pressing, especially in resource-rich countries, such as Russia and the Central Asian countries (Azerbaijan, Kazakhstan, and Turkmenistan). Russia, which has the largest share of power generation capacity (43 percent), is supposed to face 51 percent of the projected costs for the whole region (World Bank 2010). Without such investments, the biggest electricity importers (countries in the Balkans, Slovenia, and Turkey), which have already faced brownouts and blackouts, would not be able to obtain sufficient supply.

From costs to tariffs

Prices, regulations, and investments determine the costs of the sources of energy. For this report, we estimate that, for the overall region, these costs equate to 12.5 U.S. cents/kWh for electricity to cover technical costs and 16 U.S. cents/kWh for the EU-MSs countries, to take into account of some of the social costs of energy production). For gas the cost for the region of US$560/1000 m^3 (that is, US$16.70/GJ) is used. Adopting a common standard allows us to obtain a broad-brush pattern though we cannot take into account local specificities that are likely to result in country-specific cost recovery levels. As our framework indicates, most countries fix their tariffs at levels below those that would guarantee them cost recovery, thereby subsidizing the price households pay for energy. In 2009, the latest year for which we have data, only Turkey had tariffs already above cost recovery. Hungary was almost exactly at cost recovery on the basis of our cost recovery standard, which, for EU MSs, already includes a portion of the environmental costs.

If tariffs were set equal to our regional cost recovery standards, households across countries would experience price shocks of different magnitudes.[9] In most countries, the shock would be significant, resulting in an average increase in the share of household budgets spend on energy of

Increase in the Share of Household Expenditures Spent on Energy and Energy Shares before the Increase

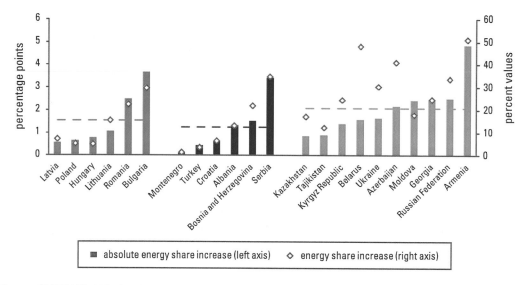

Sources: ECAPOV, World Bank estimates.

1.5 percentage points (that is, 14 percent) among EU MSs, 1.2 percentage points (that is, 13 percent) among CPCs, and 2.1 percentage points (that is, 30 percent) among EPOC countries (figure 5). Overall, the increases would range from 1.3 to 51.9 percent across all countries in the region. Figure 5 also captures the variation in the weight of energy spending in household budgets across countries in the region.

Different groups of households would be affected differently by these price shocks. Our analysis does not show a general distributional pattern indicating whether, in all cases, richer or poorer groups would be affected if prices moved instantly to cost recovery levels. Yet, even where poorer groups are not the most affected, poverty could increase significantly. We estimate, for example, that, in the EU MSs, poverty could increase by 5 to 30 percent depending on the country. In addition, energy poverty—defined as the share of households that spend a significantly high portion of their budgets (10 percent or more) on energy—would rise substantially. While, in our simulations, the poorer groups are not always those experiencing the highest increases in energy poverty, our results show high increases in energy poverty among the poor in EPOC countries.

In this report, the standard distributional analysis has been enriched by a new measure of energy stress, which is defined by the significance of the effect of a large shock, where a large shock is defined either in absolute terms (we adopt the equivalent of 100 kWh per month at pre-shock prices) or in relative terms (we consider increases of the energy share of more than 150 percent of the median). Looking at energy stress, we aim to identify groups that, whether rich or poor, might have a particular stake in opposing a move to cost recovery because they would feel significantly affected. The measure of absolute energy stress gives us some predictable results, with higher incidence in countries where there is an increase from a low base, especially among large consumers. The greatest incidence of absolute energy stress is found in EPOC countries. A focus on relative energy stress identifies some interesting patterns. Seven countries show uniform impacts so that no household can be classified as vulnerable according to this criterion. The cases of Serbia and Turkey offer an interesting contrast on how those uniform patterns manifest themselves. In both cases, there is no relative energy stress because the increase in the budget shares of all households is contained within 150 percent of the median. In Serbia, however, the average budget share almost doubles, while, in Turkey, it is almost unchanged.

Policies that influence affordability

Three broad sets of policies that influence affordability are identified in our framework: subsidies, sectoral policies, and social protection. Subsidies through the tariff system are pervasive despite significant reforms in the energy sector since transition. The most common way of implementing these subsidies in practice is through the tariff structure and, in particular, through lifeline tariffs.[10] These are block tariffs designed so that the price for the bottom block of consumption is considerably lower than the average tariff (and production costs). Lifeline tariffs offer the benefit of high coverage of the poor if the poor are mostly connected. The leakage to the nonpoor is low in poorer countries (Lovei et al. 2000). Note, however, that, while a rising block structure is often motivated by the need to subsidize basic consumption for the poorest, most tariff structures in the region are not calibrated to ensure that the average tariff equates with cost recovery, so that what varies across blocks is more the extent of the subsidy than whether there is a subsidy or not.

While lifeline tariffs (or, more generally, tariff structures that subsidize an amount of energy that is considered a basic necessity) have played an important role in cushioning the impact of the shift to higher residential tariffs over the last decade, the magnitude of the subsidies that they absorb appears unsustainable at a time of heightened fiscal pressures. Subsidies absorb an estimated 2.3 percent of GDP on average, ranging from 0 (in Latvia) to 12 percent (in Tajikistan) across countries. Even the few countries in the region with rich endowments of energy resources are starting to question whether they might invest the large resources absorbed by subsidies more effectively.

Universal subsidies through the tariff system appear as an expensive way of protecting consumers both because they represent recurrent costs and because they are universal and therefore also reach individuals who may not need support in paying their bills. This is illustrated in figure 6, which presents an approximate distribution of the implicit benefit of the subsidies dispensed through the gas and electricity tariff. This is an approximation because it equates the value of the subsidies with the difference between the cost recovery price and average tariffs, while most countries have more complex tariff structures.[11] In this simplifying framework, households benefit from the subsidy in proportion to their consumption, so that wealthier households tend to be the main beneficiaries of the subsidy. The analysis is nonetheless interesting because it shows a regressive pattern often driven by the distribution of gas connections, which is higher in urban areas and in richer areas. The pattern is reversed in Russian Federation where wealthier households rely more on district heating (excluded from the analysis in figure 6) than on gas. If implicit subsidies on district heating were included together with those on electricity and gas, a similar regressive pattern would appear.

Besides being costly and inefficient because the benefits leak to higher income groups, subsidies are also unsustainable because the developments in the energy markets, coupled with the need to start planning for significant investment in the sector, suggest that energy costs are going to continue increasing. To avoid passing such an increase along to house-

FIGURE 6
The Targeting of the Implicit Subsidy on Electricity and Gas, by Quintile

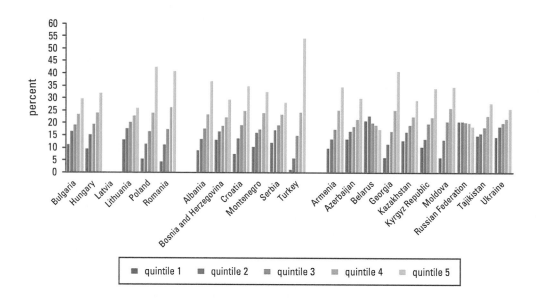

Sources: ECAPOV, World Bank estimates.

holds would require ever greater subsidies. Continuing to shelter consumers through subsidies to the sector might therefore be a vanishing
luxury for most countries.

Sectoral Policies

A subset of policies in the energy sector allows households to diversify
their energy consumption and increase their energy efficiency so as to
adapt to a higher tariff environment. Figure 7 illustrates the significant
differences across countries and income groups in energy spending patterns, which crucially depend on the modalities of heating available to
households (in particular, whether they rely on gas or district heating).
Investment in infrastructure and housing is therefore a key factor in

FIGURE 7

**Estimated Energy Consumption in Europe and Central Asia per Household with Positive
Electricity or Gas Expenditures**

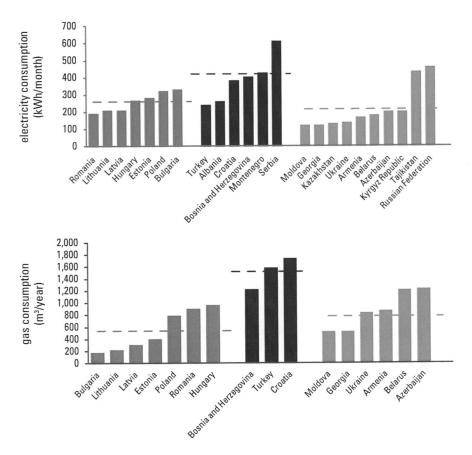

Sources: ECAPOV, World Bank estimates.

shaping consumption patterns and the possibilities for households to substitute across energy sources. In this respect, the countries of the former Yugoslavia in the CPC group stand out because district heating and gas are not provided on a large scale, thereby making most households reliant on electricity for heating. With the exception of Albania, all countries in this group consume significantly more than the regional average for electricity (more than twice the average in the case of Serbia and the former Yugoslav Republic of Macedonia).[12] Helping households manage their demand for energy by adapting their consumption patterns to a context characterized by higher prices is going to require significant investments to modify this infrastructural stock.

The need to help households transition to behaviors characterized by lower consumption has important distributional implications. Poor people, on average, allocate higher shares of their energy budgets to electricity relative to other groups because they tend to have less access to alternative sources such as district heating or gas, especially in rural areas. While the rural poor might be able to rely on wood to keep their energy budgets in check, especially if the wood is self-collected (the environmental implications of such a strategy aside), poor households in urban areas, where housing stocks are difficult to retrofit to use different energy sources, might be the most vulnerable to energy increases. In addition, if metering or energy supplies are not specific to the household, limiting consumption levels might be difficult. These concerns are supported by evidence showing that energy consumption is quite price inelastic, particularly among poorer households, and that energy consumption patterns have remained stable even if tariffs are increasing. In Armenia, for example, a substantial increase in gas and electricity prices over the last decade in the absence of sources for heating other than gas has translated into an increase in the energy share at the expense of food and health care.

The role that the type of infrastructure available plays in shaping household vulnerability to price increases, particularly among the poor, is well illustrated by a comparison of Hungary and Poland, two countries with some of the highest energy poverty rates in the region. In Hungary, the poorest households spend almost 20 percent of their budgets on energy, and there is a significant gradient across income groups, with the richest quintile spending 13 percent of their budgets on energy. In Poland, there is a broadly similar spending pattern across all quintiles, at about 14 percent. The type of utility available to provide heating helps explain these differences: in Hungary three quarters of the population report owning gas burning stoves, while only 16 percent have access to cheaper central heating (25 percent for the top quintile and 7 percent for the bottom quintile). In Poland, in contrast, the share of households with access to district heating is 37 percent (51 percent for the top quintile and 19 percent for the bottom), with 50 percent of the households reporting that they own a gas burning stove.

More comprehensive and sustainable measures are needed to help households adapt to a new high tariff environment, particularly in a context such as Eastern Europe and Central Asia, where households are still extremely inefficient in using energy. A number of initiatives and programs have helped households manage their demand by increasing energy efficiency, which represents a long-term solution to ensure energy affordability. These promising schemes can be scaled up and extended to all countries in the region, as discussed in a parallel report (World Bank 2012). While quick gains are possible with relatively limited outlay, it is likely that the bulk of the interventions aimed at fully retrofitting buildings and making them more energy efficient will require a long-term investment plan.

To give a sense of the payoffs of this type of intervention, we consider policy scenarios whereby the simplest sources of energy inefficiency are addressed (for example, basic insulation, caulking of windows, and so on), a step that should be possible with a relatively small outlay per household and that could still lead to as much as a 10 percent reduction in energy demand. The scenarios show that as much as a 2 percent reduction in the average energy share could be achieved through such an intervention and that the benefits could be highest for the lowest income groups because these are the groups that typically allocate a higher share of spending to energy. The gains would be most significant in the EPOC countries, which, as a group, are also the most energy inefficient.

Social Protection

Other than through generalized tariff subsidies, countries typically also have social protection programs aimed at helping vulnerable households pay their energy bills (energy-related social assistance, ESA). In some countries, these programs are large (for example, in Ukraine, privileges account for almost one-fifth of overall social assistance spending, and 0.45 percent of GDP) and aim to serve categories identified as deserving rather as needy. Though the coverage of these programs in the ECAPOV database is relatively limited, our assessment of the coverage, targeting performance, and generosity of ESAs shows that programs that are means tested typically have better targeting (that is a higher share of resources goes to poorer groups), but show lower coverage. Qualitative evidence highlights how administrative costs might also limit the take-up of these targeted programs by beneficiaries. Categorically targeted programs generally have much higher coverage, especially if the list of eligible groups is extensive, but they often lack in targeting, because eligibility status is not linked to income. These programs would also perform poorly in a post–tariff-increase scenario, wherein a number of new potential target groups might be seen as deserving of protection.

Given the large expected impact of an increase of household tariffs to attain cost recovery, there is a need for more effective policy solutions to address the social cost of further tariff increases. Resorting to means test-ing seems almost unavoidable so as to reduce the fiscal strains that other-wise would be inflicted on government budgets. The experience of the last decade points to new directions for improving the effectiveness of existing programs and offers examples of a number of innovations. These include reaching those most in need by strengthening the targeting of benefits and consolidating multiple programs in a common delivery mechanism, supported by investments in the development of appropriate delivery systems. The introduction in Moldova of a new means-tested energy benefit linked to the targeting mechanism for social assistance of last resort (LRSA), but with a higher eligibility threshold is a good exam-ple of how new programs can gradually replace older categorical ones in a country. Other delivery mechanisms relying on a common targeting system are also possible, such as the provisions in Poland for the delivery of energy discounts to all LRSA beneficiaries directly through their energy bills.

There are two main challenges to the expansion of means-tested ESAs throughout the region. The first has to do with delivery mechanisms. In some countries, particularly the poorer EPOC countries, poverty is exten-sive, while the delivery systems for social protection are not yet in place or are not on a scale that would allow aggressive implementation of higher tariffs to reach cost recovery without adding significantly to the burden on the budgets of the poor. While the overall direction of reforms would remain the same, the transition away from tariff-based subsidies might last longer or be more difficult to implement than elsewhere. A second challenge to the shift to targeted ESAs is offered by our simula-tions, which show that compensation does not come cheap. Even restrict-ing the compensation to the poor only—an option that might not be wise given the burdens faced also by the middle class in many countries—could require more than 1 percent of GDP for energy programs alone in the poorest countries in the region. In most countries, even this limited goal of compensating only the poor for the energy shock would require doubling the costs of existing ESAs; in Serbia, for example, this would require as much as the entire budget of the existing LRSA. The costs would be particularly high in countries with a high poverty incidence. In Armenia, for example, compensating all the poor would require 2.7 percent of GDP on ESAs alone. In most countries outside the EPOC, budgets would increase significantly if one were to focus on other groups such as lower-income households under energy stress.

These policy scenarios make it clear, therefore, that transfers alone cannot be used to guarantee energy affordability even if only to some subset of the population. Furthermore, because social assistance measures represent recurrent expenditures and do not help address the problem at the root, there is scope for complementing them with more extensive measures supporting energy efficiency.

Moving Toward Implementation of an Integrated Policy Agenda

The policy agenda put forward by this report seeks to balance the need to respond to fiscal pressures and environmental concerns on the one hand and the concerns about social impact and the political economy of reform on the other. Because the fiscal costs of maintaining current tariff structures in the face of upward pressures on the costs of energy are unsustainable, the scale of the price shock on households entailed in any move to reach cost recovery calls, in most countries, for both improved ESA and improved demand management tools. Different segments of the population would be covered by different tools: targeted social assistance measures would cater for the needs of the bottom end of the distribution, while incentives to increase efficiency would help all households manage their demand more effectively. As figure 8 shows, by focusing on all the factors that affect household vulnerability to energy tariff increases, one may free up fiscal resources that are currently absorbed by untargeted subsidies through the tariff system.

Would such an agenda be feasible? Through simple policy scenarios, we have explored the fiscal feasibility of the policy choices many countries in Eastern Europe and Central Asia are currently facing. In the counterfactual of a continuation of the status quo, countries would spend up to 4.5 percent of GDP every year to maintain current tariff levels and provide universal subsidies to all residential users. Given the large amount of resources that are currently absorbed by energy subsidies, our scenarios show that most countries would realize fiscal savings by focusing on both targeted ESAs and investments in energy efficiency for all households. We estimate these gains to be over 1 percent of GDP for almost half of the countries in the region (figure 9), though the estimates vary significantly across countries and are clearly approximations.[13] There are three important qualifications to be made about these figures. One is that alternative counterfactuals based on expectations of higher energy prices

FIGURE 8

Lower Subsidies Open Fiscal Space for Greater Investment in Sectoral Policies and Extended Support for Vulnerable Groups

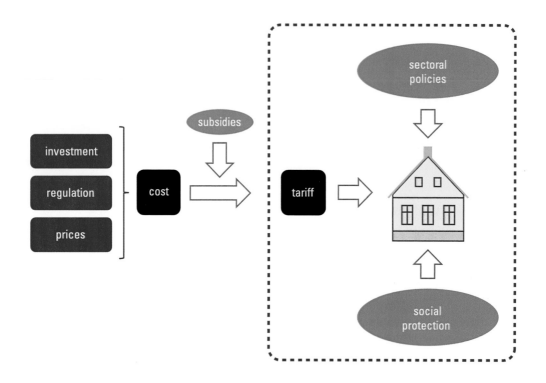

in the future would further increase the estimates of fiscal benefits from adopting this integrated agenda. The other is that the costs of sectoral policies that would increase energy efficiency are extremely difficult to estimate and could be significantly higher than what we have simulated. These costs, however, unlike subsidies and expenditures on ESAs, would represent capital expenditures as opposed to recurrent costs. Even if imperfectly captured in our scenarios, these interventions could significantly reduce household energy demand. Finally note that in these scenarios, in line with the rest of the report, EU MS raise the price of electricity to 16 U.S. cents per kWh to start incorporating the social costs of energy production—this results in additional fiscal benefits, which are particularly large in the case of Bulgaria and Romania. Similar measures could also be introduced by other countries down the line, particularly those that are closer to EU accession.

While this integrated policy agenda is fiscally feasible, the heterogeneity of countries across the region that this report documents in terms of

FIGURE 9

Estimated Net Gains from Removing Subsidies, Compensating Poor Households, and Implementing a Basic Energy Efficiency Program

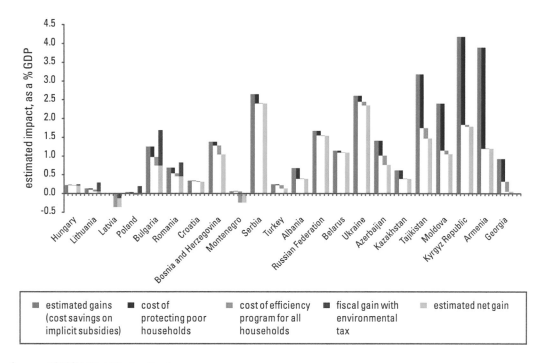

Sources: ECAPOV, World Bank estimates.
Note: estimates are given as a percentage of GDP.

the characteristics of energy sectors, poverty, and energy poverty and the characteristics of social assistance systems means that the countries are not in the same position in terms of starting to implement such an agenda. The transition from tariff-based subsidies to joint investment in demand management measures and targeted energy social assistance benefits needs to be phased in according to the effective capacity of these measures to cushion the price shock and help households adapt. In particular, as mentioned above, not all countries have targeted social assistance programs in place that are capable of ensuring appropriate coverage at the lower end of the distribution, and those that have good targeted programs might still need to extend the coverage to make the programs more effective policy tools. Similarly, demand management measures, once the easy gains have been achieved, might require significant, protracted investment.

Transitional measures might therefore be needed to start reaping the benefits of greater efficiency, while the country moves toward implementing this agenda. The scope for transitional measures varies widely across countries and can operate at many levels, from calibrating payment modalities to match household needs more closely to revising the subsidy structure. As an example of the former, in countries in which noncollection has subsidized consumers for a long time, stricter enforcement of payment could be accompanied by an effort to ensure that households can afford to renegotiate their arrears and to link this explicitly to improvements in the quality of service. Similarly, the introduction of payment modalities that allow households to smooth their energy bills throughout the year and therefore avoid falling into arrears during the months when more energy is needed for heating could remove some of the stress that households face. Examples of this second type of intervention include the introduction of seasonally adjusted tariffs that would maintain the subsidy, but only during the coldest months of the year, or adjustments in the lifeline tariffs such as a decrease in the size of the first block or the recalibration of the whole tariff structure to ensure that the costs of energy are covered even if the first block remains subsidized. This last type of intervention might be effective especially in the poorer countries in the region, where leakages to the nonpoor are more limited and where, despite low tariffs, energy poverty is already high. Similar transitional measures might apply also in countries that do have delivery systems for social assistance, but with limited coverage, such as in the case of some CPCs. The extent to which the measures can be effectively implemented, though, might be limited by elements of the EU *acquis communautaire* (or the way elements of the EU acquis have been translated into national legislation): this applies in particular to limits to cross-subsidization across different consumer groups, which can eliminate the possibility of adapting lifeline tariffs.

In conclusion, this report highlights that countries face a difficult balancing act between fiscal and environmental concerns that call for raising energy tariffs to lower fiscal burdens and curb household consumption and concerns for the affordability of energy and the political economy of unpopular reforms. Our analysis shows that focusing on a new wave of reforms, one characterized by the gradual reduction of subsidies to the energy sector and stepped up investment in demand management and protection for the poorest groups, can help countries thread this difficult path while realizing fiscal savings. Specific policy recommendations need to be tailored to the circumstances of each country. A separate set of case studies (covering Albania, Armenia, Romania, Serbia, and Tajikistan) will detail the challenges that various countries are facing in the reform process.

Based on the findings in this report, however, commonalities emerge across groups of countries. Some broad recommendations are therefore possible, as follows:

- In the EU MSs, electricity and gas prices are the highest in the region, and more than 50 percent of the population can be considered in energy poverty (that is, spend more than 10 percent of their total expenditures on energy).[14] These high tariffs reflect the fact that the move to market pricing in energy is, by and large, concluded, though new pressure to internalize environmental costs are emerging. Electricity as a share of total expenditures is more than twice as high as gas and central heating in most countries.[15] The price increases required to reach cost recovery, including the environmental cost, is estimated at 38 percent for electricity and 25 percent for gas. We simulate that the adoption of these increases would raise the total energy share from 12.5 to 14.0 percent, on average, and that 60 percent of the population would be deemed energy poor. The poverty impacts of these price increases in some countries will be nontrivial (ranging from 0.4 in Poland and Hungary to 6.9 percentage points in Bulgaria). In terms of sectoral policies to increase efficiency, this group of countries has already made significant improvements over the last decade. Also, social assistance programs are generally quite developed and show good coverage of the bottom quintile. This offers a good basis for delivering additional benefits to compensate lower-income groups for the removal of subsidies. The case of Romania, which recently abolished a central subsidy for district heating utilities and extended the coverage of a targeted benefit for district heating users, is a good example of the relative ease of implementing this type of reform once the systems (and the political will) are in place.

- In the CPCs, unit prices for energy are slightly lower than in the EU MSs, and 39 percent of the population is in energy poverty.[16] Electricity is by far the largest energy source of this group of countries, with gas and central heating almost nonexistent (except for gas in Croatia and Turkey and central heating in Serbia). On average, households spend 5.6 percent of their budgets on electricity alone. The reform agenda in the energy sector needs to be deepened, and an electricity price increase of at least 30 percent can be expected. As these countries get closer to EU accession, additional pressures to raise tariffs will arise from the need to internalize the environmental costs of energy production. Raising tariffs to reach cost recovery would increase the energy share from 9.2 to 10.4 percent and would raise to 46 percent the share of the population in energy poverty. There is great heterogeneity in terms of poverty impacts, ranging from a negligible increase in Montenegro and Croatia to a 2 percentage points increase in Albania and a 6.9 percentage points increase in poverty incidence in Serbia. While there are examples of successful programs to increase energy efficiency in specific circumstances (for example, in public buildings), overall energy efficiency is low. In most of the countries in this group, social assistance is well targeted, but there is a need to extend coverage to make social assistance a more effective policy tool. Efforts to put in place better social assistance systems are currently being undertaken in many of these countries, but, while the systems are being improved, transitional measures might be needed to ensure the affordability of energy for the most vulnerable. Albania is a good example of ongoing reforms to social assistance that would facilitate addressing the impacts of higher energy prices in the future. Changes to the block structure (the reduction in the size of the first block) offer an easily implementable transitional solution to reduce the fiscal burden of energy subsidies and eliminate some of the incentives that have led to a rise in energy consumption by households across the income distribution.

- Finally, EPOC is quite a heterogeneous group of countries; many countries in the region have not yet started to reform the energy sector, while others are well advanced. Overall, electricity and gas prices remain far from the level of cost recovery.[17] Despite the low tariffs, energy poverty is already at 34 percent, driven by the high poverty rates in some of the CIS countries. Households typically spend more on electricity than on gas, and central heating represents a significant share of the energy budget in half of the countries (Belarus, Kazakhstan, Moldova, Russia, and Ukraine).[18] An increase in electricity and gas prices to cost recovery (which could amount to up to three times the present price in some countries) would have a large impact on the energy share (which would rise from 9 to 11 percent) and on energy poverty (which would rise to 42 percent of the population). The poverty impacts due to tariff increases are on average the highest of the region ranging from 1.7 percentage points in Georgia to 5.9 in Armenia and 6.3 in Azerbaijan. This rather diverse group of countries is heterogeneous also in terms of the possible solutions to cushion the impact of higher tariffs. Energy efficiency tends to be low, particularly in countries that are resource rich, though some countries have tried to introduce programs to increase residential energy efficiency (for example, Tajikistan's efficient light bulb initiative). In terms of social assistance, this group includes countries with large, but untargeted programs that are not effective in reaching the most vulnerable groups (for example, Ukraine), countries that have already implemented significant reforms to move from such a system toward a unified system to deliver both LRSA and energy benefits (Moldova), and low-income countries without targeted social assistance programs that might be unable to deliver direct energy subsidies to a large proportion of vulnerable households in the medium term (for example, Kyrgyzstan and Tajikistan). While Moldova offers an example of how a unified targeted system can be built over time, it seems likely that, in poor countries without appropriate social assistance programs in place, transitional measures such as redesigned lifeline tariffs might continue to offer the most effective solution to ensure energy affordability for the poor in the immediate future.

Endnotes

1. A number of temporary programs were announced to address the strain that the high heating bills would cause on household budgets. Examples include the bill-paying holiday for poorer groups declared in Serbia or the distribution of energy vouchers to all households that took place in Georgia.
2. The EU MSs are the countries in the region that joined the EU in 2004 (the Czech Republic, Estonia, Hungary, Latvia, Lithuania, Poland, the Slovak Republic, and Slovenia) and 2007 (Bulgaria and Romania).
3. The average share of electricity spending ranges from 1.6 to 7.3 percent, and the average share of gas spending ranges from 0.2 to 5.1 percent of the household budget.
4. Note that the importance of energy and gas sources is quite different for the household sector relative to the country as a whole. At the moment, coal, gas, and oil account for more than 90 percent of the fuel mix in Eastern Europe and Central Asia. Even if oil now accounts for a small share of the inputs in the power sector, its international price is key as a determinant of other internationally traded primary energy products, notably, natural gas and coal. Over half of world oil production is traded. Gas markets are complex: even within a single country or region, different pricing arrangements might be in place depending on small or large uses.
5. Because the costs of district heating are location specific and not available in a consolidated database, the possible distributional implications of an increase in gas prices are discussed only in methodological appendix C.
6. EUMSs followed a "big bang" strategy with dramatic and sudden increases, partly moderated by existing safety nets. Such strategy brought significant hardship for large sections of households though it started paying off within a 2-3 year time span (WB 2012b).
7. These are three EU MSs (Estonia, Lithuania, and Poland), two Balkan countries (Albania and Bosnia and Herzegovina), and six EPOC countries (Armenia, Azerbaijan, Belarus, Moldova, Turkmenistan, and Uzbekistan). High reliance on hydropower for energy generation, as is the case in Latvia, Georgia, the Kyrgyz Republic, Tajikistan, and, to a much smaller extent, Albania, is accompanied by specific challenges, particularly those related to the seasonality of electricity production.

8. Energy intensity is defined as total energy consumption per unit of GDP. At an energy intensity level of 1.0, each 1 percent change in economic growth will be accompanied by a 1 percent change in energy demand (World Bank 2010).

9. Note that, as detailed below, we are considering a higher cost recovery standard for EU MSs.

10. In addition electricity companies have sometimes used non-collection or tolerance of high levels of technical losses (often due to illegal connections) as a way of subsidizing consumption. According to EBRD (2010) for example, the average collection rate for electricity could be very low, such as in Uzbekistan (54 percent in 2006), Azerbaijan (64 percent) and Albania (76 percent in 2008).

11. In reality, countries tend to use block tariffs; so, by focusing on the difference between cost recovery and average tariffs, we obtain a rough approximation of the distribution of the benefit. The overall size of the benefit can, however, be estimated correctly.

12. Note, however, that the rather limited group of households in these countries that have access to gas consume significantly more gas than, for example, households in the EU MS.

13. Overall, these are rather conservative estimates. While they assume that ESAs could be scaled up at no administrative cost and that resources could be perfectly targeted to the poor, they do not factor in the energy-saving effects of the energy efficiency measures discussed above. In other words, savings could be realized even if the protracted investment in energy efficiency that would be required to bring down consumption took time to materialize.

14. The respective prices in the EU MSs are 14 U.S. cents/kWh and US$16.5/GJ in 2008/09.

15. Average budget shares are 5.1 percent for electricity and 1.9 and 2.8 percent, respectively, for gas and central heating, except in Latvia and Lithuania, where the central heating share is the highest energy share.

16. The respective prices in the CPCs are 12 U.S. cents/kWh and US$13.5/GJ.

17. The respective prices are 6 U.S. cents/kWh and US$5.6/GJ, with high subregional variation.

18. Electricity represents 3.1 percent of household budgets, while gas represents 1.8 percent.

References

EBRD (European Bank for Reconstruction and Development). 2010. Transition Report 2010. London: EBRD.

Lovei, L., E. Gurenko, M. Haney, P. O'Keefe, and M. Shkaratan 2000. "Maintaining Utility Services for the Poor — Policies and Practices in Central and Eastern Europe and the Former Soviet Union."

World Bank. 2010. "Lights Out: The Outlook for Energy and Eastern Europe and Central Asia." World Bank, Washington, DC.

———. 2012. "Energy Efficiency in ECA — Lessons Learned from Success Stories." World Bank, Washington, DC.

CHAPTER 1

Introduction

Energy prices are key for the economy given energy's central role both as an intermediate input and as part of final consumption. Fiscal pressures and environmental concerns call for an increase in residential energy tariffs throughout the countries of Eastern Europe and Central Asia, despite the heterogeneous nature of the energy sectors in the region. Current tariff levels, which are possible in most countries only thanks to large subsidies to the energy sector, are not sustainable, and many countries will have to shift to tariffs that cover fully the economic cost of energy generation and distribution—and increasingly will have to cover also the social costs of that generation. Additional pressures on residential tariffs will arise from the costs of upgrading the capital base of the energy sector in the region if a lights-out scenario is to be averted (World Bank 2010).

Evidence ranging from microeconomic data to cursory looks at the press points to the difficulties that the most vulnerable will face in affording energy if governments in the region act on these pressures. Because these reforms are also likely to affect the middle class significantly, the political feasibility of reforms can be questioned unless appropriate ways of cushioning these impacts can be devised. These concerns are all the more serious in a region where the weather and the legacy of past infrastructural investment pose a serious cap on the ability of households to manage their energy demand.

Policy makers in the region are increasingly unable to put off a balancing act between these competing claims: fiscal and environmental concerns on the one hand, affordability and political economy concerns on the other. This report argues that, while challenging, the reforms needed can build on much that has been achieved in the last decade in improving the effectiveness of social assistance systems and increasing energy efficiency.

This is the first report to assess, at the microlevel, the distributional impact of raising energy prices on households in a comparable way across the entire region. It uses a unique database of standardized household surveys that covers countries in the region (the ECAPOV database). The focus of the analysis is network energy, particularly electricity and gas, though reference is made, as appropriate, to other sources of household energy. Fuel used for transport is not part of this analysis.[1] The policy insights that this work offers are complemented by detailed case studies that illustrate how to adapt these overall messages to the specificities of different country policy environments.

This report is motivated by a concern for the strain that household budgets are under whenever energy tariffs are increased. Its aim is to investigate who is affected, how, and what can be done to cushion these impacts through socially, environmentally, and fiscally sustainable solutions. Even a casual look across countries in the region shows that higher tariffs are associated with higher shares of household budgets devoted to energy (see figure 1.1 for the case of electricity), pointing to the difficulties that households in the region face in managing energy demand in a context of higher tariffs. Because households in the region are reeling from the protracted crisis, the prospect of further pressures on their bud-

FIGURE 1.1
Electricity Price and Electricity Share of Total Household Expenditures

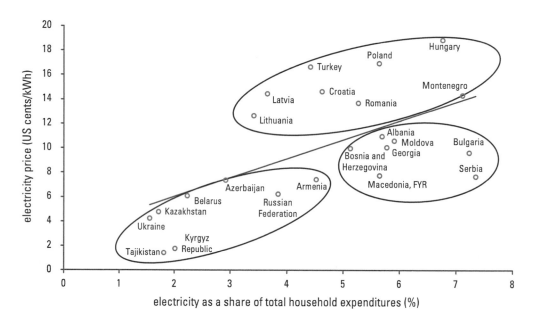

Sources: ECAPOV, World Bank estimates.

gets in an environment of inelastic energy demand clearly causes concern.

Figure 1.1 also highlights the dispersion around an average relationship, suggesting that country characteristics, including policies, greatly affect that relationship.[2] And, despite this dispersion, the figure shows some broad similarities across groups of countries.[3] European Union (EU) countries are clustered at the higher end of the tariff distribution, while Eastern Partnership and Other Commonwealth of Independent States (CIS) countries (EPOC) are at the low end. The western Balkans and Turkey, which we collectively define as Candidate and Potential Candidate countries (CPCs), are placed somewhere in between these two extremes.[4]

Why Give a New Look at a Well-Researched Issue?

The concerns of this report are certainly not new: many countries have already gone through significant reforms over the last couple of decades (box 1.1). Yet, the present economic juncture for the region brings back into the spotlight the issue of subsidies to the energy sector and calls for progress on this reform agenda. Recently, for example, calls for the abolition of energy subsidies have been at the center of the G-20 policy agenda (G20, 2011).

This report offers the first opportunity to analyze concerns about the distributional impact of such measures in a comparative perspective for the whole region, thanks to the availability of a unique database of standardized household surveys (the ECAPOV database). Because of our comparative perspective, the report findings represent a broad-brush approximation to be complemented by more in depth case studies. The adoption of a common cost recovery standard, for example, does not do justice to local-level specificities, but is meant to capture broad patterns across the region.

Note that a major body of work, especially over the last decade, has grappled with energy sector reform (World Bank 2010; EBRD 2010) or with the social sustainability of those reforms involving energy tariff increases (Lovei et al. 2000; Lampietti et al. 2007; Komives et al. 2005; UNDP 2011). These studies have helped identify and clarify the nature of the policy options to address the distributional consequences of the reforms, particularly of lifeline tariffs—tariff-setting mechanisms that ensure that small users (as a proxy for poor households) pay less than the full cost of energy—and of transfers (earmarked or not).

The policy analysis in this report adopts this set of tools as a starting point and gives it a new look by taking into account recent developments

BOX 1.1
Energy Affordability over Two Waves of Reforms in the Energy Sector

Reforms in the energy sector have broadly occurred in two waves, characterized by different ways of reconciling business needs with affordability among domestic customers.

The first generation of reforms in the 1990s focused on moving toward market systems. Energy laws were passed; independent regulators were established; and the process of liberalization and privatization started in the majority of the countries. By the end of the decade, 11 countries out of 29 had established an independent regulator, and 9 had unbundled generation transmission and distribution. The unbundling of once natural monopolies was facilitated by technological advances that allowed the decentralization of corporate control without jeopardizing the coordination of supply functions. It became possible to build separate smaller entities of what used to be a large-scale investment, and, by granting third party access to transmission, the power sector was opened to private sector participation. During this first wave of reforms, industrial tariffs rose significantly, while household tariffs were kept in check by cross-subsidization. This responded to concerns for energy affordability at a time of rapid changes and heightened household vulnerability and was possible because the fall in internal demand had left spare capacity in the system. This model, however, did not allow the funding of proper maintenance and the renewal of distribution and generation facilities. Over the decade, the quality of energy supply, particularly electricity, deteriorated, resulting in widespread blackouts and other disruptions in service.

A second wave of reforms at the turn of the new decade sought to address the need to finance new infrastructural investments and meet rising demand. As utilities removed cross-subsidization between industrial and residential customers, the policy focus was on ensuring energy affordability for the poor through block tariffs. Based on the correlation between energy consumption and income, the tariff structures were adjusted to cover the consumption of basic levels of energy at the below-cost recovery level. These tariff structures often resulted in high leakage to nonpoor customers, but, in countries with high connection rates, provided good coverage of the poor (Lovei et al. 2000).

Growing fiscal pressures and environmental concerns are now laying the basis for a third wave of reforms characterized by declining subsidies to the energy sector and by investments in demand management and other energy efficiency measures that would help households adapt to a higher price environment, while ensuring that vulnerable consumers continue to have access to affordable energy.

Source: Besant-Jones 2006.

in the region. Three developments in particular stand out and influence our analysis:

- Fiscal pressures, heightened by the ongoing crisis, have made lifeline tariffs unaffordable for many countries.

- There is a new momentum in reforming social assistance systems throughout the region because many countries need to reach the most needy more effectively, while addressing budget deficits.

- The energy sector has changed significantly, partly as a result of the reforms that have been implemented over the decade. Energy markets have changed both at the international level and the national level, and market forces are playing a much greater role today than they did a decade ago. The region has also undergone a significant transition in energy use (World Bank 2012b), and the interest in energy efficiency remains high, driven both by the EU goals for cutting emissions and awareness of the high payoff from such investments (box 1.2).

In light of these new developments and the findings of the empirical analysis on the substantial impact of the tariff increases needed for large parts of the distribution in many countries and not only the poor, the report puts forward an expanded set of policy tools to ensure energy affordability for different groups of households. Implementing these policies to ensure energy affordability while cutting subsidies to the sector amounts to a third wave in policy reforms for the sector, a complex and messy new wave of reforms, but, nonetheless, one that will be hard to postpone.[5]

BOX 1.2
High Payoffs of Investing in Energy Efficiency

Recent studies have shown the potential for significant reductions in energy usage by investing in energy efficiency. McKinsey's (2009) report on energy efficiency in 2009 showed the potential for net present value positive investments to reduce carbon emissions or, in other words, the savings as a result of consuming less energy over time exceed the cost of the energy efficiency investment. The Electric Power Research Institute's technical study (EPRI 2009) identifies achievable energy efficiency measures (for buildings and other sectors) that should reduce the annual growth rate in electricity consumption as forecasted by the U.S. Energy Information Agency by 22 to 36 percent between 2008 and 2030. The European Commission, in its communication on the Energy Performance in Buildings Directive, estimated that the improvements mandated would reduce final energy consumption by 11 percent. The countries in the region that are EU MSs must implement the EU rules, first adopted in 2002 and revised in 2009, that require certificates of energy performance for all buildings sold or rented and the target of "very high energy performance" for all newly constructed buildings by 2020. The World Business Council for Sustainable Development has created a model for energy efficiency that predicts reductions in energy use by up to 60 percent by improving energy efficiency in buildings and appliances globally.

Despite these high estimated benefits, building owners contribute to the energy paradox, whereby investments to improve energy efficiency in buildings that will repay themselves through future reductions in energy expenditure are put off. Market and coordination failures behind this paradox call for policy interventions to align individual and societal incentives and to bridge the constraints that prevent building owners from taking advantage of these high payoffs.

Sources: McKinsey 2009; EPRI 2009; World Business Council for Sustainable Development 2009.

The Analytical Framework

This report adopts a simple framework to characterize the challenge countries face in balancing affordability versus fiscal prudence and environmental constraints in setting household energy tariffs. The framework, summarized in figure 1.2: Analytical Framework , distinguishes the factors determining the technical cost of energy from those that affect energy affordability for households. Affordability (or its converse, vulnerability to tariff increases) depends on the way technical costs are translated into tariffs (that is, the extent of subsidies that the energy sector receives), how sectoral policies shape demand patterns, and the social protection measures available to support energy affordability.

A variety of factors—represented on the left-hand side of figure 1.2 as prices (that is, the combination of international prices and country exposure to them), regulation, and investment—determines the technical cost of energy.[6] The degree of subsidization of energy production and distribution affects the way these technical costs are translated into household tariffs. Chapter 1 discusses how, at a time of significant fiscal pressures

FIGURE 1.2
Analytical Framework

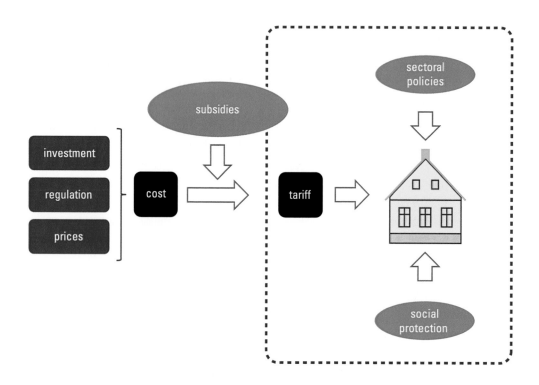

and with pressures for the cost of energy to go up, protecting households from rising costs through implicit subsidies might be a vanishing luxury.

Even difficult policy choices such as raising household energy tariffs need not result in undue stress on households. Indeed, energy affordability for households (or, conversely, the vulnerability of households to tariff increases) is affected not only by the tariffs, but also by household demand patterns, the means they have to manage demand, and the type of social protection measures available to support energy affordability. Governments therefore have two powerful policy levers to help households adapt to the new environment: helping households adapt their consumption patterns through investing in energy efficiency and providing protection from the increase to the most vulnerable groups. The consumption patterns illustrated in chapter 3 show the importance of past infrastructural investment in determining both current household consumption levels and patterns and the options for diversification households face. This helps put in context both the challenges households face in adapting to a higher tariff environment and the need for significant investments to ease such an adjustment. The need for more immediate relief, such as through transfers for poorer groups emerges in chapter 4, which, while showing that the welfare impact of increasing household tariffs to cost recovery is significant for large segments of the distribution, also illustrates how difficult it might be for those poorer groups to cope with the shock.

Because energy efficiency is the subject of a parallel report (World Bank 2012a), our discussions of the policy toolkit focuses mostly on social assistance, a sector in which a number of reforms aimed at improving effectiveness are ongoing (chapter 5). As shown in the policy scenarios in the final chapter, however, transfers alone cannot guarantee energy affordability. While maintaining the current tariff levels would require often prohibitive amounts of resources, which we estimate can absorb up to 4.2 percent of gross domestic product (GDP) a year, targeted transfers alone would still require significant amounts of resources and not provide a sustainable solution because social assistance measures represent a recurrent expenditure. Investing in energy efficiency has the potential to help much broader segments of the population manage their demand and thereby lower their vulnerability. Given the longer time frame required for these measures to be implemented, however, it is important to design strategies that integrate intervention in both areas to ensure a socially sustainable transition to a lower carbon economy.

Note that, based on similarities in the policy environments, the report identifies policy recommendations for the three broad groupings of countries we adopt (EU MSs, CPCs, and EPOC). This initial broad-brush picture will be complemented by more detailed case studies that delve into the specificities of the countries selected and their policy framework to identify feasible policy responses.[7]

Endnotes

1. For a recent analysis of oil prices and their expected impact on the region, see World Bank (2011).
2. The share of electricity expenditure in overall household budgets, plotted along the x-axis of figure 1.1, ranges from 2 percent in Kazakhstan, the Kyrgyz Republic, Tajikistan, and Ukraine to more than 7 percent in Bulgaria, Hungary, Montenegro, and Serbia. Average electricity household tariffs also vary significantly across the region. At the time of data collection, a kWh of electricity cost 17.2 times more in Hungary than in Tajikistan. If we look at a closer comparison, average tariffs in Montenegro stood at 186 percent of neighboring Serbia's.
3. This report adopts a classification of countries in Eastern Europe and Central Asia that reflects their relationship to the EU, that is, EU member states (EU MSs); CPC countries refers to the countries in the western Balkans (Albania, Bosnia and Herzegovina, Kosovo, the former Yugoslav Republic of Macedonia, Montenegro, and Serbia) and Turkey; and EPOC countries, including countries in the CIS and Georgia.
4. Turkey is closer than other countries in this group to EU member states in terms of its distance from cost recovery and its share of energy spending on electricity.
5. Implementing such an agenda would have important political economy implications. While a detailed treatment of these aspects is outside the scope of this report, an updated look at these issues is provided by Commander (2011).
6. These, of course, change over time, and policies can explicitly be devised to influence them (for example, by investing in renewable sources, countries can change their exposure to international energy prices), but, at any given time, they can be considered predetermined and technical as opposed to policy variables.
7. An essential feature of the case studies is the possibility of incorporating technical details such as the estimated level of cost recovery for different energy sources, specific to each country, as well as the exact tariff structure for the main utilities (electricity, gas, and central heating) that are currently approximated through average residential tariffs.

References

Besant-Jones, J. E. 2006. "Reforming Power Markets in Developing Countries: What Have We Learned?" Energy and Mining Sector Board Discussion Paper 12, World Bank, Washington, DC.

Commander, S. 2011. "The Political Economy of Energy Subsidies." With Chiara Amini and Zlatko Nikoloski. Unpublished paper.

EBRD (European Bank for Reconstruction and Development). 2010. Transition Report 2010. London: EBRD.

EPRI (Electric Power Research Institute). 2009. "Assessment of Achievable Potential from Energy Efficiency and Demand Response Programs in the U.S." EPRI, Palo Alto, CA.

G20 2011. Cannes Summit Final Declaration, Communiqué, November 4, http://www.g20-g8.com/g8-g20/g20/english/for-the-press/news-releases/cannes-summit-final-declaration.1557.html

Komives, K., V. Foster, J. Halpern, and Q. Wodon. 2005. "Water, Electricity and the Poor: Who Benefits from Utility Subsidies?" World Bank, Washington, DC.

Lampietti, J. A. 2007. "People and Power: Electricity Sector Reforms and the Poor in Europe and Central Asia." World Bank, Washington, DC.

Lovei, L., E. Gurenko, M. Haney, P. O'Keefe, and M. Shkaratan 2000. "Maintaining Utility Services for the Poor -- Policies and Practices in Central and Eastern Europe and the Former Soviet Union."

McKinsey & Company. 2009. "Unlocking Energy Efficiency in the US Economy." http://www.mckinsey.com/Client_Service/Electric_Power_and_Natural_Gas/Latest_thinking/Unlocking_energy_efficiency_in_the_US_economy.aspx.

UNDP (United Nations Development Programme). 2011. "Energy and Communal Services in Kyrgyzstan and Tajikistan: A Poverty and Social Impact Assessment." UNDP Bratislava Regional Centre, Bratislava.

World Bank. 2010. "Lights Out: The Outlook for Energy and Eastern Europe and Central Asia." World Bank, Washington, DC.

———. 2011 "Rising Food and Energy Prices in Europe and Central Asia." World Bank, Washington, DC

———. 2012a. "Energy Efficiency in ECA-- Lessons Learned from Success Stories." World Bank, Washington, DC.

———. 2012b. "ECA Low-Carbon Growth Report." World Bank, Washington, DC.

World Business Council for Sustainable Development. 2009. "Energy Efficiency in Buildings: Transforming the Market."

CHAPTER 2

Costing Energy: Prices, Subsidies and Household Tariffs

Despite significant reforms in the energy sector since the transition, countries have continued to subsidize energy sectors, and protecting consumers from rising costs has been one of the major objectives. At a time of heightened fiscal pressures, such subsidies appear unsustainable. Even the few countries in the region with rich endowments of energy resources are starting to question whether they might invest the large resources absorbed by subsidies more effectively. This chapter provides an overview of the extent to which countries have already progressed on the path of reforms and of the factors that suggest that further increases in costs are likely over the medium term. Developments in the energy markets and in the institutional environment, coupled with the need to start planning for significant investment in the sector, suggest that continued efforts to shelter consumers through subsidies to the sector might be a vanishing luxury. Other, more sustainable ways of ensuring energy affordability are therefore needed.

A Decade of Rising Tariffs

Figure 2.1, figure 2.2 and figure 2.3 illustrate the trends in household electricity tariffs over the past decade (similar patterns apply to gas tariffs, illustrated in annex figures 2.15-2.17). Two main elements are worth noting:[1]

- First, there is a common rising trend starting in the middle of the decade. From 2001 to 2010, electricity tariffs increased by more than 90 percent in every country examined except Armenia, Bosnia and Herzegovina, and Ukraine. Much of the increase happened beginning in 2003. Gas prices increased even more rapidly, for example, from

FIGURE 2.1

Evolution of Electricity Tariffs for Residential Users in Real Terms, EU MS

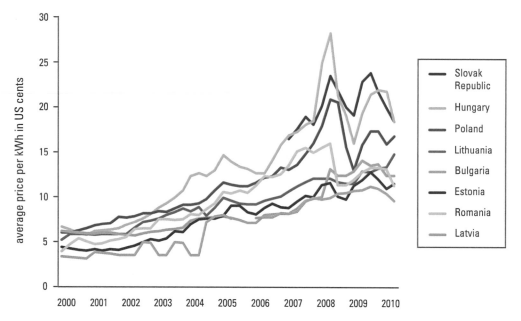

Source: ERRA Tariff Database.

FIGURE 2.2

Evolution of Electricity Tariffs for Residential Users in Real Terms, CPC

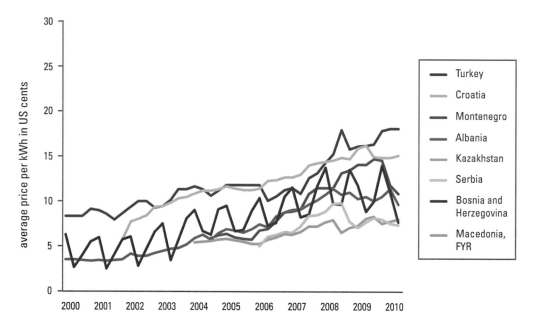

Source: ERRA Tariff Database.

FIGURE 2.3

Evolution of Electricity Tariffs for Residential Users in Real Terms, EPOC

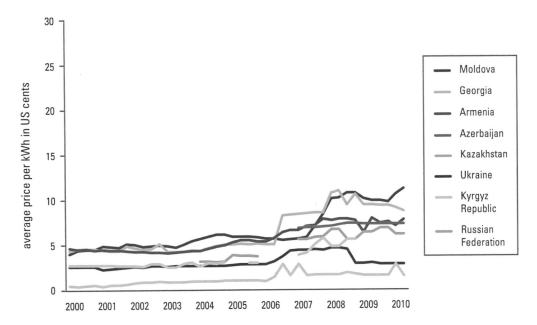

Source: ERRA Tariff Database.

US$4.70/GJ in 2000 to nearly US$20.00/GJ in 2010. In all countries, gas prices more than doubled over the decade.

- Second, there is increasing dispersion in electricity tariff levels. The differences across groups of countries became more accentuated over the period. In 2002, the average electricity tariffs were only 6 U.S. cents per kWh for countries that are now in the EU and 3.4 U.S. cents per kWh in EPOC countries. In contrast, as of the last quarter of 2009, the cost of a kWh of electricity for household consumption varied more than 14 times across the region, from 1.6 U.S. cents in the Kyrgyz Republic to 23.4 U.S. cents in Slovakia. The variation was 7.5 for gas (from 2.6 U.S. cents per GJ of gas heat in the Russian Federation, to 19.4 U.S. cents in Lithuania). In 2009, EU MSs had much higher energy tariffs than EPOC countries (on average, 17.2 U.S. cents against 6.6 U.S. cents per kWh for electricity; US$16.50/GJ against US$6.30/GJ for gas), while the CPCs adopted tariffs with prices somewhere in between (on average, 12 U.S. cents per kWh; US$14.70/GJ for gas).

As a result of this differential performance, tariffs ended up recovering different proportions of the established cost recovery standards (figure 2.5). We adopt a regional standard for cost recovery of 12.5 U.S. cents/ kWh for electricity to cover technical costs and 16 U.S. cents/kWh for the EU-10 countries (box 2.1), to take into account environmental costs,

BOX 2.1

Estimating Electricity Cost Recovery Levels for the Eastern Europe and Central Asia Region as a Whole

Determining cost recovery levels for different sources of energy requires detailed calculations at the country level. Different methodologies can be adopted depending on the cost recovery concept being applied. For example, short run marginal cost estimates take as a given the existing power generation capacity. These estimates increase with quantities consumed, as increasingly more expensive generation plants are brought into production. To the limit when the entire generation capacity has been used the short run marginal cost shoots to infinity, as additional consumption by one user is possible only by rationing consumption by other users.

Adopting Long Run Marginal Cost (LRMC) as a basis for tariff setting avoids such variability. LRMC is defined as "the incremental cost of all adjustments in the system expansion plan and system operations attributable to an incremental increase in demand that is sustained into the future".[2] By definition this is a forward looking pricing system as it is based on estimates of future capital costs rather than the historical costs of building existing generation capacity. Estimating LRMC requires forecasting demand and the least costs investments needed to satisfy it, based on detailed information on the size, timing, type of generation system, an optimal fuel mix of sources and the location of plants, in addition to the transmission and distribution assessments required to reach final customers.

As this type of calculation was well beyond the scope of this report, we relied on modeling developed by World Bank (2010) to estimate the cost of electricity generation: "as a rule of thumb, the long-run marginal cost of generation will be 6.5–7.5 U.S. cents per kWh (excluding costs associated with transmission and distribution). This estimate is based on construction of a gasfired combined cycle power plant and assumes a gas price of $250–$300 per thousand cubic meters" (p. 101). Considering that the cost of gas has risen since those estimates, we consider a price of $440 per thousand cubic meters (based on gas prices in Central Europe at the time of writing) as the basis for our LRMC for electricity. In addition we include the latest available information on equipment as a basis for this estimate. We can therefore estimate the LRMC for electricity to amount to 9 U.S. cents per kWh for generation, 1.5 U.S. cents for transmission and 2 U.S. cents for distribution. Figure 2.4 illustrates the cost structure that we adopt, and how it changes depending on gas prices.

These estimates should clearly be taken as indicative, as they are sensitive to a number of assumptions such as on the price of gas (which varies significantly by country), the type of technology used etc. More efficient equipment, for example, would result in cost savings in terms of energy production. Yet this regional cost recovery estimate is a useful tool to benchmark countries against a common standard. Finally, note that in addition to the LRMC and our estimates of costs for transmission and in this report, unless otherwise specified, the cost recovery level for electricity that we adopt for EU MS has been augmented by an estimate of the negative externalities of energy production of 3.5 U.S. cents per kWh. This is roughly based on existing estimates of the negative externalities related to health due to coal-fired plants in the United States.[3] Specific estimates relative to costs in Eastern Europe and Central Asia are currently not available.

Sources: Munasinghe et al. 1982, World Bank 2010.

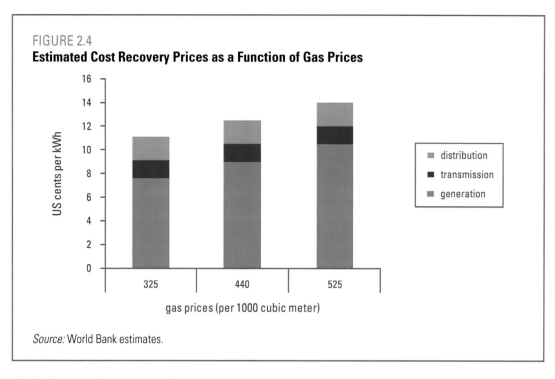

FIGURE 2.4

Estimated Cost Recovery Prices as a Function of Gas Prices

gas prices (per 1000 cubic meter)

Source: World Bank estimates.

while, for gas, these thresholds are US$560/1,000 m³ (that is, US$16.70/ GJ).[4] In 2009, the latest year for which we have data, only Turkey had tariffs already above cost recovery, while the EU MSs, CPCs, and EPOC countries were not recovering their costs. Hungary was almost exactly at cost recovery on the basis of our cost recovery standard, which, for EU countries, already includes a portion of the environmental costs (see the methodological appendix).

These trends reflect both common pressures and country-specific factors. Among the former, changes in energy markets, both global and regional, played a major role in driving up energy costs in the past. These include the tightening of global oil markets since 2000 because of strong demand globally, but especially from China; Russia's move to price gas more closely to the market within bilateral monopoly arrangements; and the increase in competition in gas markets arising from the expansion of liquefied natural gas tanker shipments.[5] Other phenomena that were important in other parts of the world, such as the development of new energy supplies, particularly in nonconventional fuels, and increases in efficiency, might have contributed to moderate energy prices in the past and are likely to play a bigger role in shaping energy costs in the region in the future.[6]

Among the country-specific factors driving the trends in rising household energy tariffs, reform efforts were a major driver.[7] Figure 2.6 shows how an independent regulator—a key institution for tariff setting—is one element of the reform package closely related to cost recovery. Note that,

FIGURE 2.5
Average Tariffs as a Share of Cost Recovery, Electricity and Gas

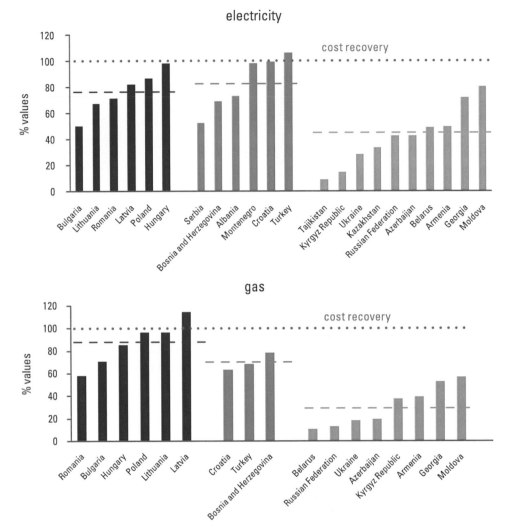

Sources: ECAPOV, World Bank estimates.
Note: For electricity, we assume a cost recovery price of 12.5 U.S. cents/kWh for CPCs and EPOC countries and 16 U.S. cents/kWh for EU MSs; cost recovery for gas is assumed to be US$560/1,000 m^3 (US$16.70/GJ).

according to the EBRD, only 11 countries in the region have a fully independent regulator; 12 are only somewhat independent; and 5 have no regulator at all.[8]

Looking generally at the reforms of the past decade, one notices that the EU MSs saw both the largest increases in tariffs over the last decade and actively introduced comprehensive reform packages through the accession process, as shown in figure 2.7, which synthesizes the progress made by countries in the region according to the EBRD index of infrastructure reform in the electricity sector. In the EU countries, power sector reform averaged 3.04 in 2000, against 3.5 in 2009.[9]

FIGURE 2.6
Cost Recovery and the Quality of Regulation

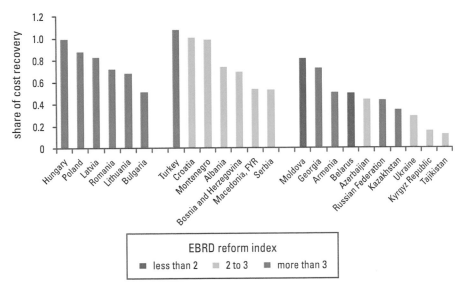

Sources: ECAPOV, World Bank estimates.
Note: The EBRD reform index ranges from 0 for no regulator to 3 for a fully independent regulator.

FIGURE 2.7
EBRD Index of Infrastructure Reform in the Electricity Sector, 2000 and 2010

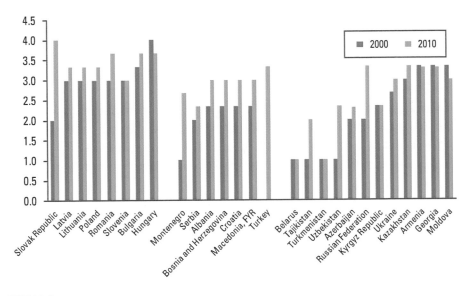

Source: EBRD 2010.
Note: The index ranges from 1 to 5 (maximum compliance with core best practices).

The CPCs, through the Energy Community (box 2.2), reached the midpoint in many reforms, such as establishing an independent regulator, allowing market access, allowing transparency in decision making, and opening up to private sector investment. According to the EBRD index, they made the greatest advances over the decade, from an average rating of 2.05 in 2000 to 2.90 in 2010.

EPOC countries, on average, have lower values of the index, indicating weaker regulation overall, with widespread government ownership and regulation of the sector. But, within this category, the picture is nuanced. Georgia, Moldova, and Ukraine, which joined the Energy Community Treaty as observers, have made more rapid progress toward open marketplace competition and regulator independence. Russia also took steps to restructure and unbundle its electricity sector.[10] The poorest performers in the region, Tajikistan, Turkmenistan, and Uzbekistan, have weak market structures; for instance, the retail market is absent, and tariff-setting procedures are opaque.

The Hidden Cost of Subsidies

As discussed above, progress in implementing reforms in the energy sector is accompanied by declines in the extent of subsidies. These were

---

BOX 2.2
Regulatory Developments Under the Energy Community (EC)

The EC is a regional organization comprising the European Community, Albania, Bosnia and Herzegovina, Croatia, FYR Macedonia, Montenegro, and Serbia. Moldova became a contracting party under the Treaty in 2010, and Ukraine in February 2011. Georgia became an observer in 2010, and Armenia's application to become an observer was recently approved.

Contracting parties in the Energy Community are already legally required to adopt the key principles of the EU gas and electricity legislation, with far-reaching obligations in the areas of market structure, wholesale and retail markets, tariff reform and affordability, and market integration. Additionally, the Energy Community conducts work in the areas of renewable energy development in the region, energy efficiency, and social issues.

The Energy Community Treaty entered into force in July 2006, aiming at creating a regional energy program that followed EU laws. The EU's third package for gas and electricity markets, which the EC placed on the schedule for implementation by 2015, requires unbundling of production and transmission, strengthened regulators, and greater transparency in network operations. Complying with the European directives and legislation will increase the cost of business during the transition period.

In 2006, the European Commission estimated that the contracting parties of the Energy Community must invest US$30 billion to enhance the electricity networks for connection with the EU grid and an even larger amount for the gas network.

Source: http://www.energy-community.org/portal/page/portal/ENC_HOME/ENERGY_COMMUNITY

certainly significant. In 2003, it was estimated that, of 19 countries considered, 9 spent more than 3 percent of GDP to cover the hidden costs of their implicit subsidies to the power sector (figure 2.8).[11] Recent estimates are available only for a smaller set of countries, but they suggest that, in some countries, at least such costs have declined. In the Kyrgyz Republic and Tajikistan, the decline has been quite dramatic (figure 2.9), though

FIGURE 2.8

Hidden Costs in the Electricity and Gas Sector, 2003

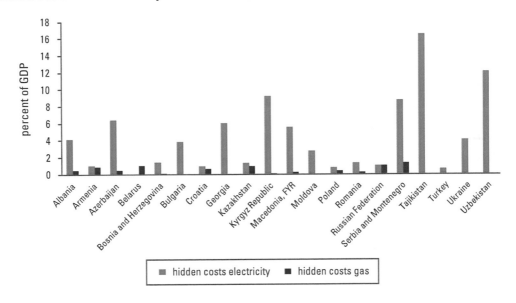

Sources: Ebinger 2006; World Bank 2011a.

FIGURE 2.9

Trends in Hidden Costs in the Electricity Sector in Selected Countries 2000–2009/10

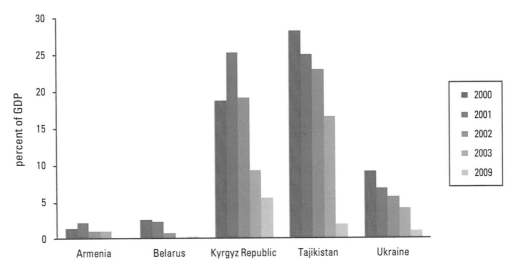

Sources: Ebinger 2006, World Bank 2011a.

the hidden costs continue to absorb more than 1 percent of GDP in Tajik-istan and nearly 5 percent in the Kyrgyz Republic. Note that it is not possible to break down how much of the estimated hidden costs is accounted for by the household sector.[12]

Signs of declining subsidies are encouraging because these subsidies are not pro-poor (box 2.3) while most countries in the region are currently under significant fiscal pressure. As illustrated in figure 2.11 and figure 2.12, most countries are facing both significant fiscal deficits and increasing government debt. Deficits, in particular, range from an esti-

---

BOX 2.3

Distribution of the Implicit Subsidy Supplied Across the Board to Households through Residential Electricity and Gas Tariffs

Under the simplified assumption of a flat tariff across quintiles, underpriced electricity and gas consumption benefits more actual users of gas and high electricity consumers, thus wealthier households. The regressive pattern shown in figure 2.10 for most countries is driven significantly by the distribution of gas connections. For example, the pattern is reversed in the Russian Federation because poorer households spend more on gas than wealthier ones and thus benefit more from the related implicit subsidy. (Wealthier households use more central heating than gas). A more comprehensive analysis using district heating subsidies would provide a regressive pattern for Russian Federation as well.

FIGURE 2.10

Distribution of Implicit Electricity and Gas Subsidies, by Quintile

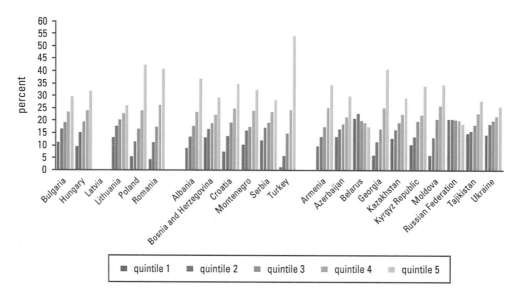

Sources: ECAPOV, Staff estimates.
Note: For countries where block or targeted tariffs ensure lower tariffs to poor households, the regressive pattern might be overestimated. However, a detailed analysis conducted in Albania using the actual block tariff structure showed a similar pattern to the one produced using the average tariff (World Bank 2011b).

FIGURE 2.11
Predicted Fiscal Balances, 2010–12

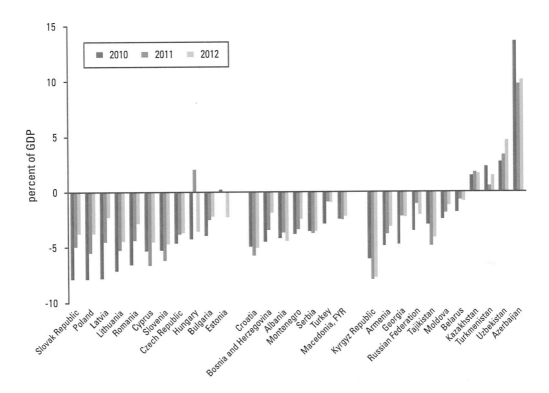

Source: IMF staff estimates.

FIGURE 2.12
Government Debt, 2010–12

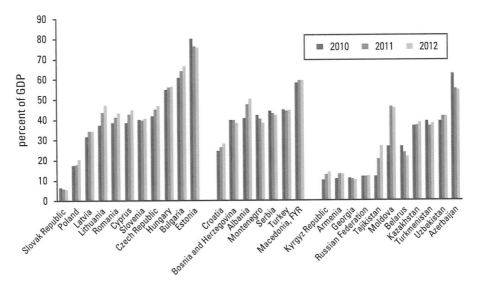

Source: IMF staff estimates.

mated 1 percent in Turkey to a 4.5 percent government deficit in Lithuania in 2011, suggesting that the fiscal space to subsidize the energy sector is limited and is likely to become even more so if the current crisis in the euro area deepens.

Looking Ahead: Drivers of Future Increases

If energy subsidies appear unsustainable at current costs, the perspective of rising costs adds to the urgency of addressing the liability that a commitment to current tariff levels would put on government budgets. Three main factors can be expected to drive energy costs in the future: the dynamics of international prices, regulatory and institutional developments, and investment needs. Of these, the evolution of international prices in the medium term is perhaps the most uncertain to predict, particularly for oil, which is a key reference price in the sector. The World Bank forecast is relatively moderate, with the average oil price at US$80/bbl in constant 2011 dollars as the long-term price, down from the current average of US$100/bbl.[13] A more dire forecast comes from the International Energy Agency, with oil prices at US$135/bbl (2009 dollars) in 2035 (under current policies), though policies to reduce emissions could moderate the growth to only US$113/bbl in real terms by 2035.[14]

Despite these uncertainties, there seems to be agreement on some basic facts: the low costs of oil that were seen until 2000 are unlikely to come back; gas prices are likely to follow demand and supply more closely than they have in the past, likely increasing their volatility with respect to the past; and, even if limited, these changes could have significant consequences. Figure 2.4 well illustrates this last point: an increase in gas prices from US$250 to US$350 per 1,000 m³ leads to an estimated increase of 14 percent in the long-run marginal costs for electricity generation from gas sources.

Regulatory developments aimed at internalizing the social costs of energy production will create additional pressures on costs. These refer to both health costs and, more recently, climate-related impacts. At the EU level, there are targets to contain both types of social costs, namely, targets to reduce or eliminate emissions of a number of toxins and pollutants that impact local air quality and human health, and targets to reduce the EU's overall greenhouse emissions (box 2.4).[15] As these social impacts are hard to quantify, it is unclear how much these regulations would impact energy costs. For negative externalities related to health, damage in the United States from coal-fired plants has been estimated at 3.2 U.S. cents per kWh.[16]

Finally, further pressures on costs are going to arise from the need to undertake massive investments over the next two decades to avoid an

---

BOX 2.4
Emissions Trading Schemes and Energy Price Impacts

Emission trading schemes place a price on the emissions of carbon dioxide (CO_2) and other greenhouse gases, as well as negative global climate externalities, and, as a result, increase the cost of generating electricity. In the case of climate-related impacts, estimates range from US$1 and US$100 per ton of carbon, depending on the models. The only current market price for carbon is the EU emissions trading scheme, whereby a ton of carbon traded at between €6 and €14.5 in 2011.

A number of factors impact the cost increases in electricity because of emissions trading schemes. First, a country's fuel mix is especially important, as countries with hydropower or gas-fired generation (Latvia relies on renewables for more than 30 percent of power generation) have lower emissions per kWh generated than countries that rely heavily on coal-powered plants (for example, Estonia and Poland rely on coal for more than 50 percent of power generation).

Second, the amount of emission allowances also impact the price. The EU's emissions trading scheme for carbon dioxide (CO_2), which entered into force in January 2005, provided many emission allowances at no cost to power generation facilities, thus mitigating cost increases. Nonetheless, anticipating having to purchase future allowances, some power producers priced in carbon costs. During the first phase of the EU emissions trading scheme (2005–07), electricity tariffs increased significantly. A meta-review of many studies showed that estimates of the increase in electricity tariffs due to emission trading varied between €1 and €19 per MWh (at a carbon price of, in general, €20 per tCO_2). These represent only the costs passed through to end users.

---

energy crunch. The World Bank (2010) argues that investments on the order of trillions are needed to face the estimated increases in electricity and primary energy consumption.[17] Over the next 20 years up to 2030, the estimated regional financial effort required to sustain production and supply amounts to US$3.3 trillion, of which US$1.3 trillion for primary energy development, US$1.5 trillion for the power sector, and another US$0.5 trillion for district heating. The growth that will spur this sharp rise in energy demand will allow part of these investments to be sustained, but will not be sufficient to finance them entirely.

Country Exposure to Higher Prices

Countries in the region not only have reformed their energy sectors and subsidize their energy sectors differently, they are also going to be differentially impacted by these new pressures on costs. Regulatory pressures, for example, are going to be highest among EU MSs and among countries that aspire to become EU MSs. Investment needs are going to be especially pressing in resource-rich countries, particularly Russia and Central Asian countries (Azerbaijan, Kazakhstan, and Turkmenistan).

Russia, having the largest share of power generation capacity (43 percent), is supposed to face 51 percent of the projected costs for the whole region (World Bank 2010). Without such investments the biggest electricity importers (countries in the Balkans, Slovenia, and Turkey) that have already faced brownouts and blackouts would not be able to get sufficient supply.

As for the exposure to international prices, it depends on the extent of reliance on imports, on the diversification of resources, and on the energy intensity, as follows:

- A few countries that are not dependent on imports will be less exposed to changes in international energy prices. As figure 2.13 shows, only five countries (Turkmenistan, Kazakhstan, Azerbaijan, Russia and Uzbekistan, in order from the least energy dependent) fall in this category. At the other end of the spectrum, a half-dozen countries rely on imports for more than 90 percent of their total energy consumption (in order from most dependent, Moldova, Belarus, Slovakia, Armenia,

FIGURE 2.13
Energy Dependency (Net Imports/Consumption)

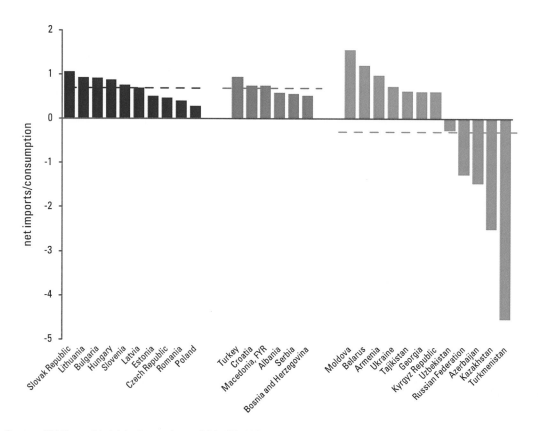

Sources: ECA Energy Model, background material for World Bank 2010.

Turkey, and Lithuania).[18] As we discuss above, some importers receive oil or gas below cost under bilateral agreements with Russia, but prices are expected to converge to European levels in the near future. This picture might also change in the future as countries become more dependent on imports. For example, only a few of the countries that are currently big users of coal have reserves large enough to shelter them from possible external shocks in the future. These include Russia, with an estimated 18.2 percent of proven world reserves, and Kazakhstan and Ukraine with 3.9 percent each.[19] In contrast, Romania has less than nine years of coal reserves left at current production.[20]

- Countries that are more diversified in terms of energy resources are likely to be less exposed to international price changes, particularly if the link between oil and gas pricing continues to weaken. Across the region, 11 countries obtain more than 50 percent of their fuel mix from one source.[21] High reliance on hydropower for energy generation, as is the case in Georgia, the Kyrgyz Republic, Latvia, Tajikistan, and, to a much smaller extent, Albania, is accompanied by specific challenges, particularly those related to the seasonality of electricity production.

- Finally, countries that use energy more efficiently, all else constant, will be less exposed to the dynamics of international markets. Since the beginning of the transition, there have been significant improvements in energy efficiency across the region, which has been brought about by the shift from heavy to light industry and commercial services (for example, box 2.5 for the case of Poland). But, as shown in figure 2.14, EPOC countries, in particular, still have the highest levels of energy intensity.[22]

Conclusions

After a decade in which household energy tariffs have been rising in most countries in Eastern Europe and Central Asia even if at a varying pace and to reach different levels, additional incentives to increase prices are on the horizon. Unlike the past, however, growing fiscal restraints are likely to limit the ability of governments to shield households by subsidizing the energy sector, and new ways to protect vulnerable consumers will have to be found.

The upward pressure on energy costs differs across countries in the region: over the medium term, EU MSs will face more starkly the need to adopt social pricing fully so as to internalize the costs of the local and global impacts of energy consumption. They will also continue to strive

BOX 2.5
Decreasing Energy Intensity: The Case of Poland

Poland decreased its final energy intensity by 46 percent between 1990 and 2008 and, today, has per capita energy demand among the lowest in the EU. Of the decline in final energy intensity, 2 percent is attributed to structural changes in the country's economy, while the remaining 44.5 percent may be attributed to energy efficiency improvement measures. Between 1997 and 2003, the residential energy efficiency index declined at an average rate of 5.3 percent per year. During this period, important policy measures were introduced, namely, pricing that reflected energy generation costs (introduced in the early 1990s), the creation of the Thermo Modernization and Renovation Fund (1998), and the introduction of technical requirements for buildings (2002). The bulk of the improvements in final energy intensity took place during the first decade of the transition as the country shifted from a centrally planned to a market economy. With strong economic recovery during the first decade of the 2000s (GDP growth averaged 4.6 percent between 2002 and 2008), the declining trend in energy consumption was reversed as the opportunities for upgrading energy inefficient components of the economy were depleted.

There is still significant potential for energy efficiency gains, especially in the building sector, which accounts for 40 percent of final energy demand. Average energy consumption in Poland is about 240 kWh/m^2, which is roughly double that of Denmark. New buildings must meet an energy usage standard of 120 kWh/m^2, and Poland is examining the feasibility of nearly zero energy buildings with energy consumption levels of 30 kWh/m^2. The transition will be driven by policy reforms already under way and will continue to evolve, including (a) removal of market barriers through the white and building certificates programs, (b) improved buildings standards, (c) low-cost financing for the residential sector, (d) improved metering and control systems, and (e) an active outreach program.

Renovating old buildings provides larger gains. A building certificates program provides renters and purchasers with information about building energy usage, creating a motive to enhance energy efficiency to raise marketability. Poland plans to provide grants of up to 16 percent of the cost and 20 percent of loans for renovations through the Thermo Modernization and Renovation Fund of PLN 200 million, with commercial bank leveraging up to Zl 1.0 billion.

These incentives are expected to support investments that will improve the efficiency of building envelopes to help the government meet its energy efficiency targets.

Source: World Bank 2012.

to diversify their sources of energy by promoting non–carbon-intensive production to raise energy security and temper the impact on the climate.

CPCs, which need to reform their energy sectors to comply with EU regulations, will have to establish or ensure the proper authority of an independent regulator, increase bill collection and payment, and maintain or gradually reach cost recovery levels. Internalizing social costs should also start featuring on the agenda.

FIGURE 2.14
Energy Intensity, or Energy Use per US$1,000 GDP, 2008

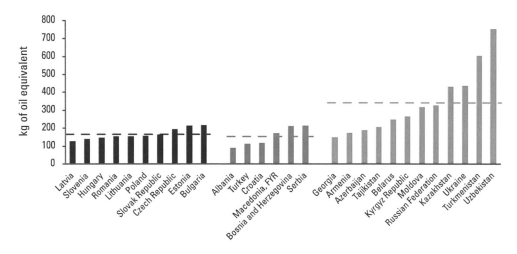

Source: World Development Indicators (database), World Bank, Washington, DC, http://data.worldbank.org/data-catalog/world-development-indicators.
Note: Energy use is calculated in constant 2005 purchasing power parity U.S. dollars.

EPOC countries face the most urgent need to continue reforms and increase tariffs to cost recovery levels, particularly countries that are not rich in energy resources, given that these are highly exposed to the downside of price increases. Increasing bill collection and payments, enhancing regulation, and boosting the efficiency of transmission and distribution systems, are the key priorities of these countries.

Endnotes

1. As discussed below, a number of factors contribute to domestic price dynamics. For the sake of simplicity, we will discuss these under the headings of prices (including international prices and country exposure to them, which, in turn, depend on resource endowments and the type of technology used to produce energy), regulation, and investments. For example, low residential electricity tariffs in the Kyrgyz Republic and Tajikistan might reflect the large reliance on hydropower, as well as lagging reforms in the energy sector.
2. Munasinghe et al. 1982 pg. 52.
3. For negative externalities related to health in the United States, damage from coal-fired plants has been estimated at 3.2 U.S. cents per kWh but there is great variation in estimates, from less than 0.5 U.S. cents per kWh to more than 12 U.S. cents per kWh. From gas-fired plants, it has been estimated that the mean damage stands at 0.16 U.S. cents per kWh (NRC 2009).
4. As discussed in the introduction, this common standard might only approximate the true cost recovery value in each of the countries, but offers the advantage of providing one common standard to benchmark countries. Note also that energy prices fluctuate, particularly that for gas.

5. As of today, coal, gas and oil account for more than 90 percent of the fuel mix in Eastern Europe and Central Asia. Even if oil now accounts for a small share of the inputs in the power sector, its international price is key as a determinant of other internationally traded primary energy products, notably, natural gas and coal. Over half of world oil production is traded. Gas markets are complex: even within a single country or region, different pricing arrangements might be in place depending on small or large uses. Innovations seen elsewhere in the world, such as the movement toward spot gas pricing is still limited in Eastern Europe and Central Asian countries because it is physically unavailable in parts of the region, largely due to reliance on Russia for all imports of gas. Note that these increasing energy costs have already pushed countries to reduce energy subsidies, as shown by the declining hidden costs discussed below.

6. In the recent past, developments in extraction techniques have significantly affected markets; for example, the U.S. market has seen decreases in gas prices due to the development of shale gas. Because of environmental concerns linked to some of these techniques, their potential adoption in EU MSs and possibly in the CPCs is still not certain.

7. As discussed below, country exposure to international prices varies depending on local endowments, making the endowments an important country-level driver of tariff dynamics in each country.

8. The indicator distinguishes between fully independent (institutional, financial, managerial, and decision-making independence), partial (some elements of independence, but not all four dimensions), and no regulator.

9. The index ranges from 1 to 5 and captures compliance with the core best practices identified by the EBRD: an independent regulatory authority, a transmission service operator and related market unbundling, nondiscriminatory network access, and a published, transparent tariff structure.

10. Russia created a wholesale market for electricity and opened generating companies to private investment. The gas sector is still dominated by Gazprom, which enjoys monopoly status for gas exports and controls nearly all Russian gas production, transmission, and distribution.

11. These were mostly EPOC countries (Azerbaijan, Georgia, the Kyrgyz Republic, Tajikistan, Ukraine, and Uzbekistan), the Balkans (Albania, FYR Macedonia, and Serbia), and EU MSs (such as Bulgaria, in particular). The hidden costs were defined as the difference between the actual revenue charged and collected at regulated prices for the service provided and the revenue required to cover fully the operating costs of production and capital depreciation (Saavalainen and Ten Berge 2004).

12. The hidden costs are calculated as a function of poor bill collection rates, excessive losses due to inefficient operations or theft from the network (in power, gas, or water systems), and tariffs set below cost recovery (defined so as to include the costs of long-run operations and maintenance and allowance for reasonable investments and for inevitably predictable losses in transmission and distribution). They are not broken down, however, by industrial and residential customers.

13. This is based on the cost of unconventional oil sands development in Canada. This price is expected to be sufficient to supply the expected moderate growth in world oil demand. There are no resource constraints into the distant future, and unconventional fuels continue to be developed, in part because of incentives deriving from high prices. Nearly all the growth in demand is expected in developing countries, as the demand for growth among members of the Organisation for Economic Co-operation and Development will likely be constrained by high prices and anticipated improvements in efficiency in the transport sector (Streifel 2011).

14. There are clearly a number of factors that will affect the true evolution of energy prices, including supply and demand conditions, the development of unconventional sources, the costs of mitigating environmental impacts, and the power of the Organization of Petroleum Exporting Countries. New technological developments akin to those that have led to horizontal drilling and shale gas and oil production could also lower costs, while drastic measures to improve efficiency could bring prices closer to their long-term costs, as happened after the second oil shock in Europe.

15. Examples of toxins and pollutants are sulphur dioxide, nitrogen dioxide, and oxides of nitrogen, particulate matter and lead in ambient air, the use of chlorofluorocarbons and other substances that deplete ozone, and major pollution from combustion plants, waste incineration plants, and other industrial installations. The targets set in 2008 seek to reduce emissions from non–EU Emissions Trading Scheme sectors (transport, housing, agriculture, etc...) by 10 percent by 2020 compared with 2005 levels, stipulating 20 percent emission reductions for the richest EU MSs and allowing up to 20 percent emission increases for the poorest EU MSs, including EU members in Central and Eastern Europe.

16. There is great variation in estimates, from less than 0.5 U.S. cents per kWh to more than 12 U.S. cents per kWh. From gas-fired plants, it has been estimated that the mean damage stands at 0.16 U.S. cents per kWh (NRC 2009).

17. These estimates are robust to a number of assumptions on the trajectory of the recovery.

18. Note that resource-rich countries, while secure in terms of their domestic energy production, might still be vulnerable to external shocks through their dependence on export earnings. For example, Kazakhstan, which exports 2.5 times as much energy as it consumes, relies on energy trade for 23.6 percent of its GDP. Azerbaijan, with an energy dependency ratio of −1.47, relies on energy trade for 44.8 percent of its GDP. In the present context, this type of macroeconomic vulnerability is likely to manifest itself in terms of volatility in export revenues.

19. These three leading countries have reserve/production ratios (indicating the length of time before coal reserves are exhausted at the current production rate) of more than 300 years (BP 2011).

20. Note that Bulgaria and Poland, which rely on coal as the major source in their fuel mix and have 82 and 43 years of domestic proved reserves remaining, respectively, already saw their share of imported coal rapidly increasing in the years up to 2010.

21. These are three EU MSs (Estonia, Lithuania, and Poland), two Balkan countries (Albania and Bosnia and Herzegovina), and six EPOC countries (Armenia, Azerbaijan, Belarus, Moldova, Turkmenistan, and Uzbekistan).

22. Energy intensity is defined as total energy consumption per unit of GDP. At an energy intensity level of 1.0, each 1 percent change in economic growth will be accompanied by a 1 percent change in energy demand (World Bank 2010).

References

BP Statistical Review of World Energy, 2011

Ebinger, J. 2006. "Measuring Financial Performance in Infrastructure: An Application to Europe and Central Asia" Policy Research Working Paper 3992, World Bank, Washington, DC.

EBRD (European Bank for Reconstruction and Development). 2010. Transition Report 2010. London: EBRD.

Munasinghe et al. 1982. Electricity pricing : theory and case studies, Washington, DC: Johns Hopkins University press for the World Bank.

NRC (National Research Council of the National Academies). 2009. Hidden Costs of Energy: Unpriced Consequences of Energy Production and Use. Washington, DC: NRC.

Saavalainen, T. and J. Ten Berge. 2004. "Energy Conditionality in Poor CIS Countries", IMF, Washington, DC.

Streifel, S. 2011. "Energy Pricing." Background note for Balancing Act, unpublished. World Bank, Washington, DC.

World Bank. 2010. "Lights Out: The Outlook for Energy and Eastern Europe and Central Asia." World Bank, Washington, DC.

———. 2011a . "Hidden Cost of Energy Supply in ECA: An Update." Background note for the ECA Low-Carbon Growth Report.

———. 2011b. "Electricity Tariffs and Protection of Vulnerable Households in Albania. Unpublished report, World Bank, Washington, DC.

———. 2012. "Energy Efficiency in ECA — Lessons Learned from Success Stories." World Bank, Washington, DC.

FIGURE 2.15
Evolution of Gas Tariffs for Residential Users in EU MSs

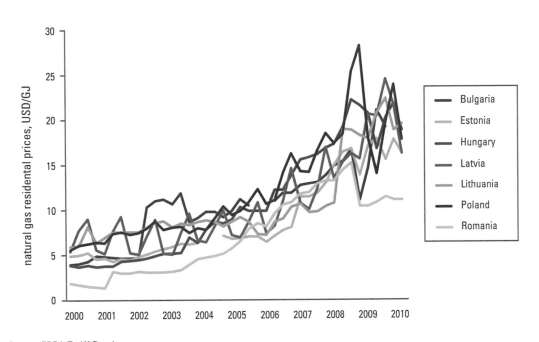

Source: ERRA Tariff Database.

FIGURE 2.16
Evolution of Gas Tariffs for Residential Users in CPCs

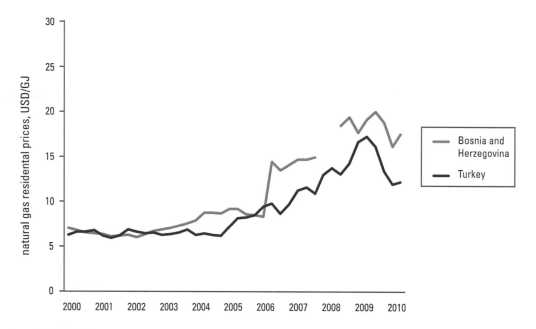

Source: ERRA Tariff Database.

FIGURE 2.17
Evolution of Gas Tariffs for Residential Users in EPOC

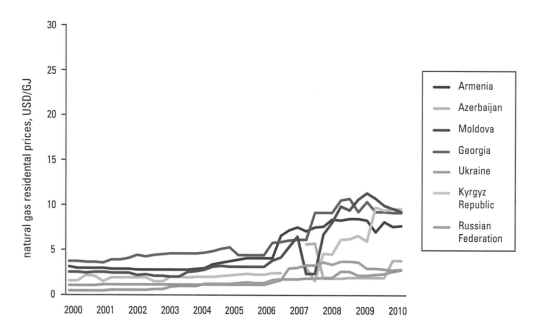

Source: ERRA Tariff Database.

CHAPTER 3

Heat and Light: Household Energy Consumption in Perspective

Household vulnerability to energy tariff increases crucially depends on overall household consumption patterns and, specifically, energy consumption.[1] This chapter explores the energy sources used by different groups of households across the region and the variations in consumption patterns and energy poverty in different contexts. Past investments in infrastructure and housing significantly condition current consumption patterns and the possibilities for households to substitute across sources of energy. Available data show that energy consumption is quite price inelastic and that energy consumption patterns have remained stable even at times of tariff increases, at the expense of other basic necessities. Helping households manage their demand for energy by adapting their consumption patterns to a context characterized by higher prices is going to require significant investments to modify this infrastructural stock. The experience of the EU MSs, which started with energy tariffs comparable with those of the EPOC countries, but now have higher tariffs and lower physical consumption of electricity and gas than other countries in the region, shows that adjustments are possible. But, if not accompanied by improvements in efficiency, the adjustments are likely to be painful.

Profiling Energy Sources

A comparison of the composition of energy spending across countries shows that electricity is the dominant energy source in the region (figure 3.1). It accounts for more than a third of recorded total energy spending in 21 of 23 countries. In the western Balkans, Belarus, and Bulgaria, electricity accounts for over 60 percent of recorded energy spending. The greatest variability in electricity spending is among the EPOC countries,

FIGURE 3.1
Share of Energy Expenditure, by Energy Type

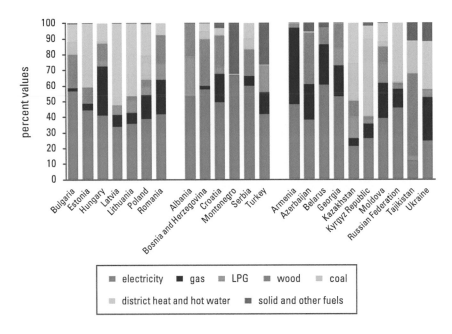

Sources: ECAPOV, World Bank estimates.
Note: See methodological appendix D for a discussion of the variables in the various surveys.

reflecting structural and infrastructure variations across this country grouping.

In fact, as highlighted by an ongoing case study on Albania, one of the key drivers of electricity spending is the availability of alternative sources of energy for heating. In households in which electricity is the main source of heating, electricity consumption is 30 percent higher than the national average. Considerably higher consumption of electricity is reported by households that do not have firewood expenditures, and the incidence of firewood use in the bottom consumption quintile decreased from 71 percent in 2005 to 54 percent in 2008. If the shift away from firewood is caused by supply constraints and not merely to changes in fuel preferences, then rising electricity tariffs are likely to be an important source of vulnerability. Notably, the incidence of electricity poverty was 17 percent in households reporting no firewood expenditures, according to 2008 data, but only 7 percent in 2005.

Gas is consumed by households in most countries and represents more than a quarter of household spending only in Hungary, Moldova, Romania, Ukraine, and Armenia, where it is the main source of heating. District heating and hot water spending varies greatly, depending on availability.[2] Households in the EU spend between 10 and 52 percent of their energy budget on central heating and hot water. The highest shares are recorded in Latvia and Lithuania, where access to this energy source is the widest in the region. Access to district heating and hot water is heterogeneous in the EPOC countries, but, even if access is widespread, as in Russia or Ukraine (70 and 40 percent, respectively), households report lower expenditures on these energy sources, most likely because they pay highly subsidized rates for district heating. The case of Ukraine has been recently examined, and subsidized gas prices, deferred maintenance, and underinvestment were found to help keep the production cost of district heating artificially low, by 50 percent of the true cost (World Bank 2011a).

Wood expenditures vary greatly across all countries, and, as discussed in the methodological appendix, it is the energy source captured the least consistently across household surveys. In our data, it accounts for 53 percent of energy expenditures in Tajikistan and around a quarter of energy expenditures in Azerbaijan, Bosnia and Herzegovina, and Bulgaria. In the CPCs, 60 to 80 percent of households use wood as their main source for heating, though their expenditures are primarily for electricity, suggesting that self-collection is the main source of acquiring the wood, and that this highly seasonal purchase is not well recorded in the current questionnaires.[3]

Finally, coal expenditures are much more localized in countries with coal production. They account for more than 20 percent of energy spending in Kazakhstan and the Kyrgyz Republic and only in Poland among EU MSs. The seasonality pattern may also hinder the appropriate capture of such expenditures (see methodological appendix D).

The importance of electricity is reflected in physical consumption levels (figure 3.2).[4] In all countries, on average, households consume more than 120 kWh of electricity per month, which is often taken as an estimate of minimum energy requirements at least in poorer countries (Komives et al. 2005).[5] Gas consumption varies significantly across the region: its importance in a comparative perspective is harder to judge because, in some countries (such as Bosnia Herzegovina), the distribution infrastructure is limited, as detailed in annex 3.1.

Price levels are an important correlate of these patterns because EU MSs that have, in broad terms, higher than average energy tariffs for both electricity and gas also have lower consumption levels, while the opposite is true in the EPOC countries (despite significant variation); the CPCs are somewhere in the middle.[6] But, besides pricing structures, infrastructure availability affects the pattern of physical consumption, as follows:

- In EU MSs and Turkey, where electricity prices are high and where alternative heating sources such as central heating or network gas are available to most households (except for Bulgaria), consumption ranges from 200 to 330 kWh/month, on average.

FIGURE 3.2
Estimated Energy Consumption in the Region

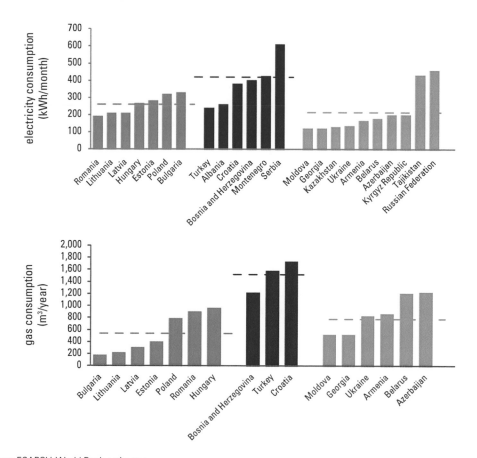

Sources: ECAPOV, World Bank estimates.
Note: The sample is households with positive electricity or gas expenditures.

- In contrast, consumption estimates are high in the western Balkans, where central heating is nonexistent or limited and where apartment buildings are mainly heated by electricity or wood. Average electricity consumption is in the higher range of 260 to 600 kWh/month, and Serbia, where only 10 percent of households are supplied with gas, has an average electrical consumption more than 2.5 times the average in the other countries.

- In most EPOC countries, alternative heating sources are available to most households, and average electricity consumption is closer to basic needs (from 120 to 200kWh/month). The exceptions are Russia, where both electricity and gas consumption are high (about 60 percent of households are supplied with gas), and Tajikistan, where electricity prices are also the lowest and where few households are supplied with gas. In these two countries, consumption levels reach 400 kWh/month.

Figure 3.3, figure 3.4 and figure 3.5 highlight differences in consumption patterns across income groups.[7] Poorer groups typically allocate a higher share of energy spending to electricity relative to richer households,

FIGURE 3.3
Energy Shares by Quintile, as Proportion of Total Spending on Energy, EU MSs

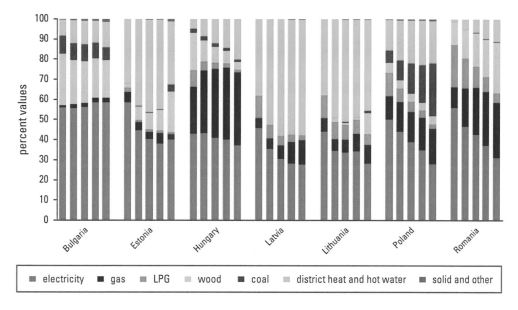

Sources: ECAPOV, World Bank estimates.

FIGURE 3.4
Energy Shares by Quintile, as Proportion of Total Spending on Energy, CPCs

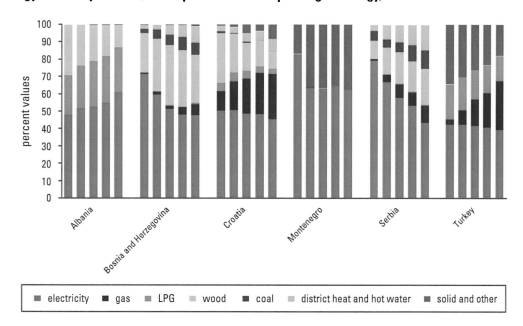

Sources: ECAPOV, World Bank estimates.

FIGURE 3.5
Energy Shares by Quintile, as a Proportion of Total Spending on Energy, EPOC

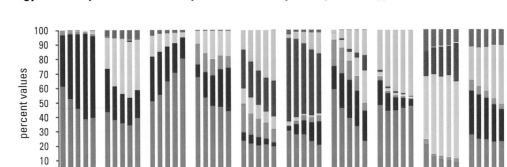

Sources: ECAPOV, World Bank estimates.

though, in a few countries (Albania, Azerbaijan, Bulgaria, Croatia, Hungary, Russia, Tajikistan, and Ukraine), the share of electricity expenditure is rather flat across groups, and, in only two countries, richer households spend relatively more on electricity (Belarus, Turkey).[8] Other energy sources such as district heating and gas are typically more widely available in urban areas than in rural areas and are thus typically used more regularly by richer groups. Qualitative evidence from ongoing case studies for this report provide useful insights on consumption and spending patterns among the poor (box 3.1). Poor households appear to be extremely aware of the costs of electricity and to be adopting all kinds of energy saving behaviors, ranging from keeping only one room of the house warm to going to bed early to using electricity only for essential tasks; cooking, for example, is an activity that it is deemed to be unaffordable with electricity.

In the EPOC countries, richer households have greater access to district heating, though there are indications from surveys in Ukraine that some poor households would consider disconnecting from district heating if prices increase.[9] Wood is also an important source of consumption across all income levels, though in a higher proportion in the poorest and rural households. Only in Belarus do richer households consume significantly less wood than poor households. In all CPCs, wood is the main source of heating, but also in Bulgaria, Moldova, Romania, and Tajikistan.

BOX 3.1
Affordability and Household Consumption Patterns: Evidence from Focus Groups in Albania and Serbia

Focus groups in Albania revealed an interesting pattern among households that are not paying their electricity bills regularly. Poor households in areas where nonpayment is common consume more energy than average. These households have a number of systemic explanations to justify the culture of nonpayment prevalent in their areas. Households that are not able to pay their bills in areas where the majority of the population are paying regularly display a different behavior. They claim that electricity is not affordable, even it is used sparingly. These households, while in arrears, try to minimize the use of electricity, and the monthly bill is a source of worry and a reminder of the extent to which they are falling into debt. These households display behaviors similar to the behaviors of other poor households that are regular in their payments: they do not use electricity for tasks such as cooking or heating, and they suggest that it is impossible to substitute away from electricity for other tasks such as lighting, refrigeration, washing machine use, or television. Many households resort to borrowing from family and friends, cutting food expenditures, or illegal connections because of their inability to pay electricity bills.

Sources: World Bank 2011b, 2011c.

'Energy Poverty' and Affordability

According to the latest estimates, country averages for household spending on energy range from 4 to 16 percent (figure 3.6). EPOC countries have the greatest variation in household spending on energy, while the CPCs are the most consistent, allocating between 7 and 12 percent. Households in Moldova and Tajikistan, among the poorest countries in the region, allocate the highest share of their expenditures to energy. Expenditure shares on energy are also high in EU MSs despite the lowest rates of poverty and highest income levels. This is consistent with the higher prices typically charged in EU countries. All EU countries are, on average, above the 10 percent cutoff we adopt to identify energy poverty (box 3.2); only Lithuania is below the 10 percent threshold and only by a small margin.

The incidence of energy poverty across the region is detailed in figure 3.7, which shows the shares of households spending more than 10 percent of their budgets on energy. This ranges from 6 percent in Belarus (which is probably underestimated because some utility expenditures are not accounted for) to 80 percent in Hungary. The energy poverty rate is high in the EU countries; the lowest is at 30 percent in Lithuania. In the CPCs, between 30 and 50 percent of households are in energy poverty, slightly less than in the EU MSs. In the EPOC countries, where tariffs are still far below full cost recovery levels, energy poverty is lower than in the

FIGURE 3.6
Household Budget Share of Energy Spending

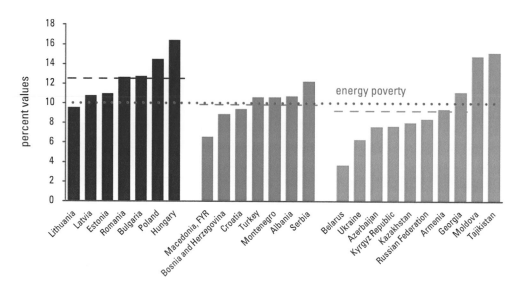

Sources: ECAPOV, World Bank estimates.
Note: Belarus energy expenditures do not include district heating because this could not be distinguished from all other housing expenditures (see methodological appendix D) and is almost completely limited to electricity expenditures.

FIGURE 3.7
Energy Poverty Rates in the Region

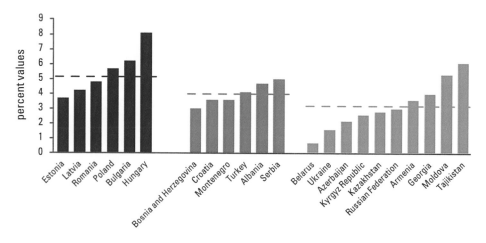

Sources: ECAPOV, World Bank estimates.
Note: The energy poverty rate is the share of households spending more than 10 percent of their budgets on energy.

BOX 3.2
Defining Energy Poverty

At its origin, the concept of energy poverty implied the inability of households to meet the physiological energy needs—for example, for heating, cooking, or lighting—with available resources. In practice, though, most definitions of energy poverty specify a resource threshold in terms of a maximum acceptable proportion of household income devoted to energy consumption.

An extensive regional study on power sector affordability in Southeastern Europe, commissioned by the EBRD in 2003, provided two examples of criteria for energy poverty, as follows:

In Hungary, energy poverty is based on three criteria: (a) the household's monthly energy expenses reach or exceed 35 percent of the total monthly household income, (b) the household's monthly heating expenses reach or exceed 20 percent of the total monthly household income, and (c) per capita income in the household does not exceed twice the lowest old-age pension amount. Thus, energy-poor households are defined in reference to a minimum income, whether they are struggling to pay bills, and whether heating bills represent a significant proportion of total expenses. An alternative approach involves a basic energy consumption threshold as well.

In Scotland, energy poverty is defined as the level at which a household would need to spend 10 percent or more of its income on all fuel and heat the home to an adequate standard of warmth. According to World Health Organization recommendations, 21°C in the living room and 18°C in other rooms should be ensured. Here, the definition focuses on what a household would need to pay to maintain adequate warmth, rather than what it actually pays.

Another method of defining energy poverty, commonly used in developing countries, is to assume that the energy poverty line is equal to the average energy consumption of those households in which overall per capita consumption reaches +/– 10 percent of the purchasing power parity US$1-a-day income poverty line. (The water poverty threshold in the United Kingdom is also defined based on the water expenditure of the poorest households.) However, for energy, this must be adjusted upward for cold countries to take account of the costs of maintaining an adequate level of heating in dwellings.

EBRD (2003) underlines that assessing electricity affordability is less straightforward than assessing energy poverty.

The European Commission's Energy 2020 strategy aims to protect vulnerable consumers, devolving the definition of energy poverty to EU MSs. The commission's working paper notes that the lack of a consensus definition for energy poverty should not be a problem per se because it allows for solutions that are adapted to national and local conditions. Thus, some countries define energy poverty as household energy expenditures that exceed a certain share or household expenditure on energy products that is a higher proportion than the national average. An alternative proposal looks at households that have difficulties making payments or are in arrears, though this is not shown to have a strong correlation with price.

Source: European Commission 2010b.

other two subregions, surpassing 40 percent only in Moldova and Tajikistan.

A disaggregation of spending by quintile shows interesting patterns across and within countries. Poorer households typically allocate a higher share of spending to energy. The pattern is not always consistent, though, especially in the CPCs; for example, in Montenegro energy spending jumps between 8 and 12 percent across income quintiles (figure 3.9). In a few cases, such as in Romania, richer households allocate a greater portion of spending to energy (figure 3.8).[10] Among EPOC countries, lower

FIGURE 3.8
Energy Spending by Quintile, as a Proportion of Total Spending, EU MSs

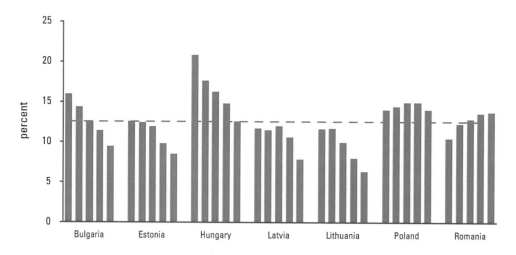

Sources: ECAPOV, World Bank estimates.

FIGURE 3.9
Energy Spending by Quintile, as a Proportion of Total Spending, CPCs

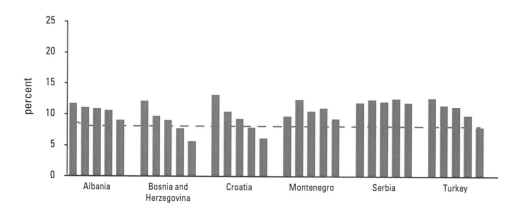

Sources: ECAPOV, World Bank estimates.

poverty rates are associated with more significant differences between rich and poor households in allocations to energy spending (figure 3.10). For example, in Russia (which has one of the lowest poverty rates among the EPOC countries), energy spending drops from 11.5 to 4.0 percent across quintiles, while, in Albania (which has the highest poverty rate in the CPC group), energy spending drops from 13 to 8 percent across quintiles. This pattern is consistent with greater pressures for subsidizing energy in countries with larger groups of poor households.

FIGURE 3.10
Energy Spending by Quintile, as a Proportion of Total Spending, EPOC

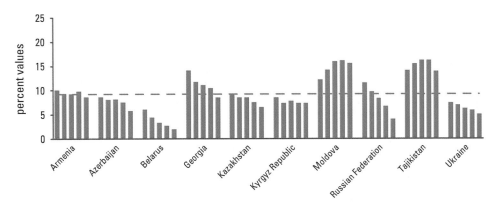

Sources: ECAPOV, World Bank estimates.

An interesting comparison is provided by Hungary and Poland. In Hungary, which has the lowest rates of poverty in the EU and the highest energy prices, the poorest households spend almost 20 percent of their incomes on energy (figure 3.8). The high rate of energy poverty in Hungary (figure 3.7) is therefore driven primarily by the high levels of energy poverty among poor households. In Poland, a comparable rate of energy poverty with Hungary reflects a broadly similar spending pattern across quintiles. The type of utility available to provide heating helps explain these differences: in Hungary, three quarters of the population report owning gas burning stoves, while only 16 percent have access to cheaper district heating (25 percent for the top quintile and 7 percent for the bottom quintile). In Poland, in contrast, the share of households with access to district heating is 37 percent (51 percent for the top quintile and 19 percent for the bottom), and 50 percent of the households report they own a gas stove.

Disaggregating the data by rural and urban areas, one finds other interesting patterns (see annex 3.2). For most EU countries, energy poverty is nearly the same in rural areas and urban areas. However, in Latvia and Lithuania, urban energy poverty is 4 percentage points greater than rural energy poverty (12 and 8 percent and 10 and 7 percent, respectively). In these two countries, district heating accounts for around 60 percent of urban energy expenditures and less than one-third of rural expenditures, making it harder for urban households to adjust to tariff increases. The weight of district heating (albeit subsidized) in the budgets of urban households is visible also in EPOC countries. In Moldova, Russia, and Ukraine, in fact, urban households spend proportionally no less than rural households (though the latter might be complementing their energy budget with wood from self-consumption, as is the case in Moldova). In the two other countries where urban households are spending proportionally more than rural ones (Armenia and Georgia), expenditures on gas seem to be behind this finding, though it is likely that the energy budgets of rural households are complemented by wood from self-consumption. Finally, in 5 of the 10 EPOC countries, rural households spend proportionally more on energy than their urban counterparts. This difference is particularly marked in the case of Tajikistan, where solid fuels represent the highest energy expenditures.

To put these numbers in context, it is useful to consider briefly the other major components in household budgets. On average, half of all expenditures go to food, 7 percent each go to transport and clothing, 6 percent cover health costs, and other categories account for between 2 and 5 percent of expenditures (see the annex).

Adjusting to Higher Tariffs

Available data show that energy consumption is quite price inelastic and that energy consumption patterns have remained stable even at times of tariff increases and at the expense of other basic necessities. Recent trends show that energy consumption patterns have not changed much (figure 3.11).

The ability of households to shift to cheaper energy sources or to cut demand is clearly limited by other factors. The physical availability of different energy sources is largely determined by network infrastructure. Similarly, housing characteristics constrain consumption adjustments, given the difficulties and costs to retrofit housing to allow for the consumption of different energy sources, the harshness of the climate in parts of the region, and the low energy efficiency of parts of the housing stock. These factors also help explain why households might have a limited ability to adjust their consumption if household tariffs increase. Available estimates put energy elasticity between −0.25 and −0.3 (for example, the average price elasticity of demand across the western Bal-

FIGURE 3.11
Trends in the Share of Energy Expenditures

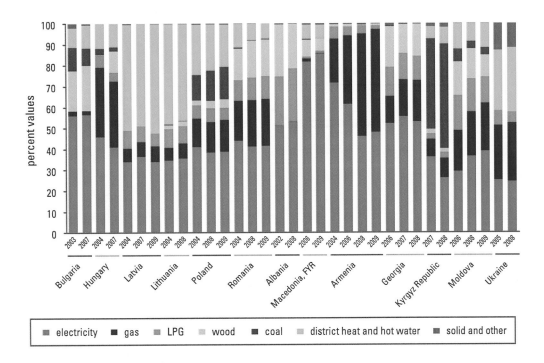

Sources: ECAPOV, World Bank estimates.

kans was estimated at −0.285 [World Bank 2009]). An important quali-fication of these country averages comes from a detailed study in Turkey suggesting that price elasticity of electricity in the short run ranges from −0.2 for poor households to −0.6 for rich households (Zhang 2011). To the extent that poorer households find it more difficult to cut energy consumption following a shock and are unable to substitute consumption to less expensive sources of energy, concerns for energy affordability in the face of tariff hikes and on the pressures they put on other items in household budgets are well founded. Indeed, the last decade has seen the energy share in household budgets increase in most countries on which data are available.[11]

The case of Armenia is particularly interesting in this respect. House-holds typically depend almost entirely on electricity and gas. Following a substantial increase in gas prices over the last decade, expenditures on gas increased from around 20 percent of total energy spending in 2004 to around 50 percent in 2009 (figure 3.12). At the same time, the share of household expenditure on energy increased 35 percent, reflecting the price inelasticity of gas consumption in the absence of alternative energy sources (figure 3.13). Households with little choice to switch to other

FIGURE 3.12
Evolution of Average Residential Gas Tariffs, Armenia

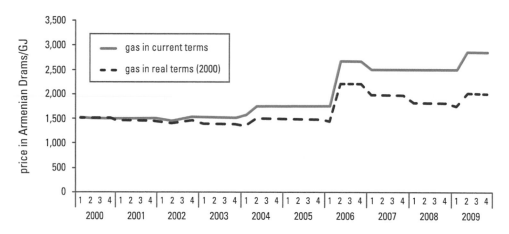

Sources: ECAPOV, World Bank estimates.

sources or energy therefore reduced spending on other goods such as food and health care. In the case of Armenia, spending on food dropped by 8 percent, and household spending on health care dropped 50 percent. Like household energy spending, transport spending also increased, by 50 percent, putting further strain on household budgets.

FIGURE 3.13
Trends in Energy Shares over the Last Decade

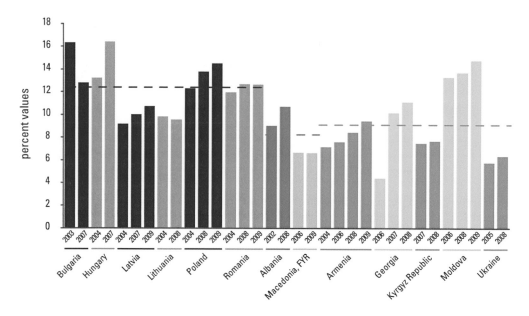

Sources: ECAPOV, World Bank estimates.

Despite the difficulties that households find in adjusting to increases in energy tariffs, particularly the poorest households, the experience of the EU MSs, which started with energy tariffs comparable with those of the EPOC countries, but now have higher tariffs and lower physical consumption of electricity and gas (see annex 3.2) than other countries in the region, shows that adjustments are possible. But, if not accompanied by improvements in efficiency, they are likely to be painful.

Conclusions

Electricity is the dominant energy source in the region, though its weight in household budgets reflects the availability of other energy sources for heating. For this reason, reliance on electricity is significant in the western Balkans, where few households appear to have access to gas. While, on average, countries in the region consume significant amounts of energy, tariff variations across the region are correlated with consumption levels. Broadly, EU MSs states, which have the highest tariff levels, also have the lowest consumption, while EPOC countries are at the other end of this spectrum with lower tariffs and higher consumption levels.

Poorer groups typically allocate a higher share of spending to energy, and, within energy spending, they allocate more to electricity relative to richer households. Other energy sources such as district heating and gas are typically more widely available in urban areas than in rural ones and, thus, are typically used more by richer groups. Country averages for household spending on energy range from 4 to 16 percent. The share of households that spend more than 10 percent on energy (our definition of energy poverty) varies significantly across the region, ranging from 15 percent in Ukraine to 80 percent in Hungary.[12] Despite higher income levels, the incidence of energy poverty is greater in EU MSs because of high tariffs. In the EPOC countries, where tariffs are still far below full cost recovery levels, energy poverty is less extensive than in the other two subregions, surpassing 40 percent only in Tajikistan, where households spend mostly on solid fuels, and Moldova, where tariffs are close to cost recovery.

High levels of spending on energy are a concern because energy consumption is quite price inelastic, and energy consumption patterns have remained stable even after tariff increases at the cost of forgoing other basic necessities, as shown by the recent experience of Armenia. The limited ability of households to adjust to higher tariffs arises because of the role of the physical availability of different energy sources (determined by the network infrastructure available) and of housing characteristics in driving the options and opportunities of households to manage their energy consumption. Poor households, in particular, might face greater constraints in adjusting their demand, raising the need to cushion the impact of a price shock on them, while investing to help all households adjust to a high-tariff environment.

Endnotes

1. The availability of government programs explicitly directed at making energy affordable for vulnerable groups—another crucial determinant of household vulnerability—is discussed in the next chapter.
2. In half of the countries, hot water is supplied as a utility. In most of them, hot water is distinct from central heating (Latvia, Lithuania, Kazakhstan, the Kyrgyz Republic, Moldova, Poland, the Russian Federation, and Turkey), while, in four of them, hot water expenditures are gathered with central heating (Croatia, Estonia, Serbia, and Ukraine). In all other countries, no hot water expenditure is reported (Albania, Armenia, Azerbaijan, Belarus, Bosnia and Herzegovina, Bulgaria, Georgia, Hungary, the former Yugoslav Republic of Macedonia, Montenegro, Romania, and Tajikistan). In all energy expenditures, central heating thus includes hot water if available. In Belarus, district heating cannot be identified from total expenditure for utilities (only electricity, gas, and other fuels are reported).
3. Questionnaires typically have a one-month recall, with a three-month recall for additional items that are purchased much less frequently.
4. These consumption levels are estimated using the ERRA database for average tariffs, which obviously represents an approximation of the true tariff structure (likely to include different blocks at increasing cost).
5. 120 kWh, which is sufficient for a few lightbulbs, a small refrigerator, and a television.
6. Bulgaria and Poland are exceptions: consumption levels are slightly above average. Households in Tajikistan pay 30 percent of the regional average for electricity and consume an estimated 430 kWh of electricity per month, 1.5 times more than the regional average; in contrast, in the Kyrgyz Republic, despite an average electricity tariff that is 26 percent of the regional average, consumption is still below the regional average; other factors, such as low-income levels, low levels of ownership of electrical appliances, and a strong dependence on coal for heating might explain this finding.
7. As discussed in methodological annex 4, income groups are proxied by quintiles of total expenditure per capita.
8. As noted by Lampietti et al. (2007), Albania and Turkey have significant nonpayment issues involving the nonpoor. Recent work in Albania confirms the existence of entire areas of nonpayment and documents how an estimated 25 percent of the cost recovery level for household tariffs reflects energy theft and noncollection. In Belarus, grid utility expenditures may be part of a global housing expenditure and thus might be excluded from the estimates of total energy spending.
9. In Belarus, district heating could not be distinguished from aggregate housing expenditures.
10. This is also the case in Moldova, where the pattern would be monotonically decreasing if wood from self-consumption were included. (See Methodological annex 4 for details on how the energy variable has been standardized across countries.)

11. In Bulgaria, total consumption has increased far beyond the inflation between 2003 and 2007 (the increase was 28 percent in constant prices). Energy expenditures only increased in line with inflation (that is by 30 percent, but resulting in no increase in constant prices). Thus, the energy share decreased. This puzzling finding could be driven by such a large increase in household welfare that households were able to decrease the burden of energy in keeping their energy expenditures stable. More research is needed to understand whether this indeed was the case.

12. We omit the Belarus energy poverty rate from this range because it is underestimated given that not all grid utilities are included in the relevant variables (see the methodological annex).

References

EBRD (European Bank for Reconstruction and Development). 2003. "Can the Poor Pay for Power? The Affordability of Electricity in South East Europe". London: EBRD.

European Commission. 2010b. "An Energy Policy For Consumers." Commission Staff Working Paper SEC (2010) 1407, final, European Commission, Brussels.

Komives, K., V. Foster, J. Halpern, and Q. Wodon. 2005. "Water, Electricity and the Poor: Who Benefits from Utility Subsidies?" World Bank, Washington, DC.

Lampietti, J. A. 2007. "People and Power: Electricity Sector Reforms and the Poor in Europe and Central Asia." World Bank, Washington, DC.

World Bank. 2011a. "Modernization of the District Heating Systems in Ukraine: Heat Metering." Unpublished report, World Bank, Washington, DC.

————2011b. "Electricity Tariffs and Protection of Vulnerable Households in Albania. Unpublished report, World Bank, Washington, DC.

————. 2011c. "Serbia Case Study." World Bank, Washington, DC.

————. 2012. "ECA Low-Carbon Growth Report." World Bank, Washington, DC.

Zhang, Fan. 2011. "Distributional Impact Analysis of the Energy Price Reform in Turkey." Policy Research Working Paper 5831, World Bank, Washington, DC.

Main Heating Sources and Access to Utilities in Eastern Europe and Central Asia

In addition to data on energy expenditures, most countries in the ECAPOV database provide information on access to main utilities such as electricity, gas, central heating, and hot water. Information on main heating sources are also available (figure 3.14). This information is highly com-

FIGURE 3.14
Access to Main Utilities

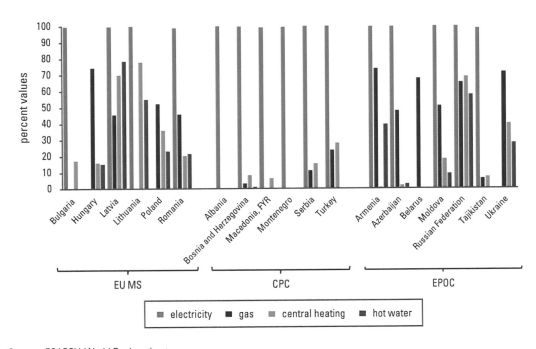

Sources: ECAPOV, World Bank estimates.

plementary and often essential to understanding data on expenditures, which, by definition, do not capture nonpayment or might capture imperfectly other uses of self-collected energy sources such as wood or highly seasonal expenditures.

Access to electricity is universal in the subregion, while district (central) heating, gas, and hot water supplies are country specific and also linked to urban-rural status.

In the EU countries, central heating is supplied to more than 80 percent of the urban households in Lithuania and Latvia and to 40 and 55 percent, respectively, of the households in rural areas. In the other EU countries, central heating is less widespread and almost exclusively concerns urban households (figure 3.15). Gas is mainly supplied in Hungary (urban and rural areas), Poland (urban), Romania (urban), and Latvia (urban). It is limited in Lithuania and Bulgaria, even in urban areas.

FIGURE 3.15
Access to Main Utilities in Urban and Rural Areas, EU MSs

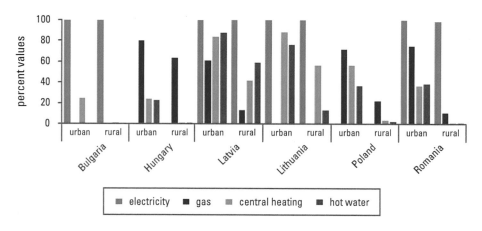

Sources: ECAPOV, World Bank estimates.

In the CPCs, households rely almost exclusively on electricity: central heating is supplied to few urban households in Turkey (39 percent), Serbia (27 percent), Bosnia and Herzegovina (21 percent), and FYR Macedonia (11 percent), and gas supply is even more limited (urban Turkey, Serbia, and Bosnia and Herzegovina) (figure 3.16).

Access to gas is better distributed in EPOC countries, where rural households are also supplied (even in a lower proportion than urban ones), except in Tajikistan, where only 6 percent of households are supplied with gas (figure 3.17). Central heating is supplied to urban households in Moldova, Russia, Ukraine, and, in a lower proportion, in Tajikistan (no data were available on Belarus). Based on reported energy expenditures, some urban households are also supplied with central heating in Kazakhstan and the Kyrgyz Republic.

FIGURE 3.16

Access to Main Utilities in Urban and Rural Areas, CPCs

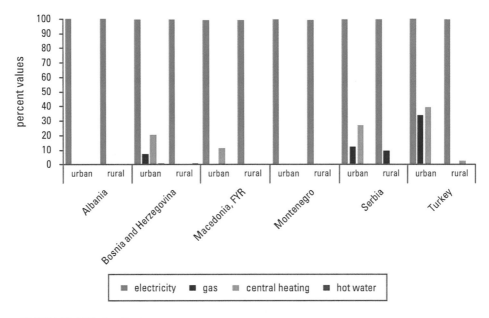

Sources: ECAPOV, World Bank estimates.

FIGURE 3.17

Access to Main Utilities in Urban and Rural Areas, EPOC Countries

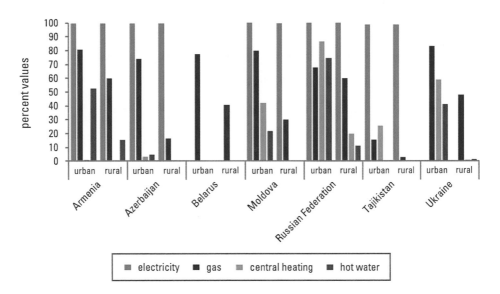

Sources: ECAPOV, World Bank estimates.

FIGURE 3.18
Main Heating Source

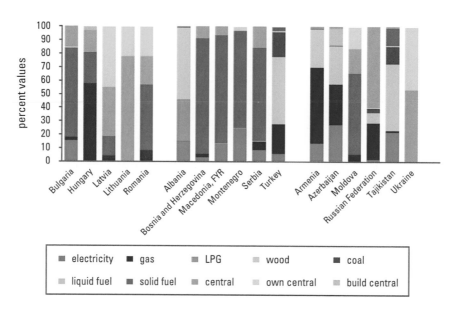

Sources: ECAPOV, World Bank estimates.

FIGURE 3.19
Main Heating Source in EU MSs, by Urban and Rural Area

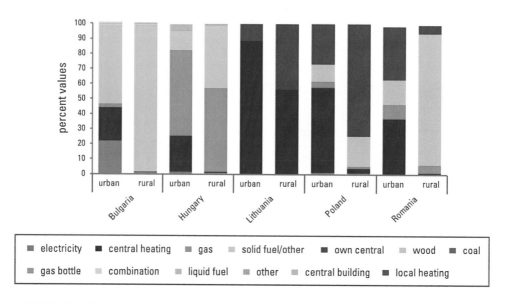

Sources: ECAPOV, World Bank estimates.

FIGURE 3.20
Main Heating Source in EU MSs, by Quintile

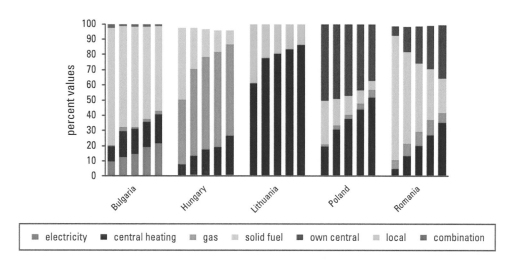

Sources: ECAPOV, World Bank estimates.

FIGURE 3.21
Main Heating Source in CPCs, by Urban and Rural Area

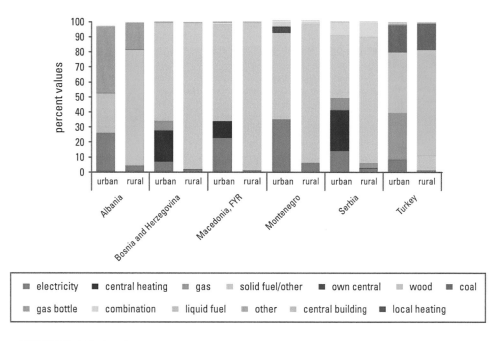

Sources: ECAPOV, World Bank estimates.

FIGURE 3.22
Main Heating Source in CPCs, by Quintile

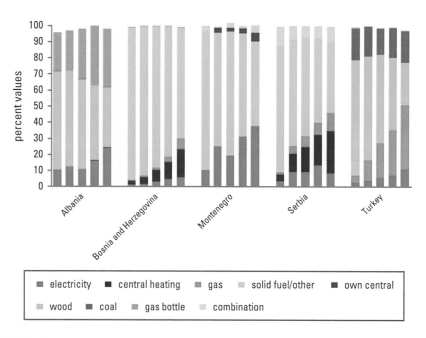

Sources: ECAPOV, World Bank estimates.

FIGURE 3.23
Main Heating Source in EPOC, by Urban and Rural Area

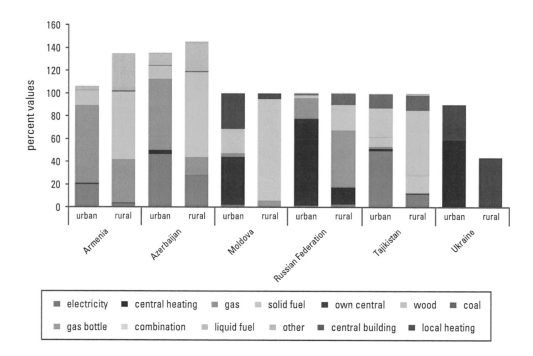

Sources: ECAPOV, World Bank estimates.
Note: In Azerbaijan, several sources could be reported. In Ukraine, only central heating (district or own) was reported.

FIGURE 3.24

Main Heating Source in EPOC, by Quintile

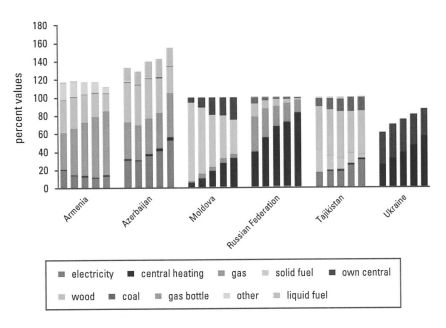

Sources: ECAPOV, World Bank estimates.

Rural-Urban Differences in Spending

FIGURE 3.25

Energy Expenditure as a Share of Total Spending, Rural and Urban Areas, EU MSs

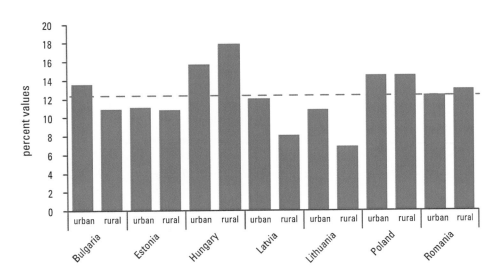

Sources: ECAPOV, World Bank estimates.

FIGURE 3.26

Energy Expenditure as a Share of Total Spending, Rural and Urban Areas, CPCs

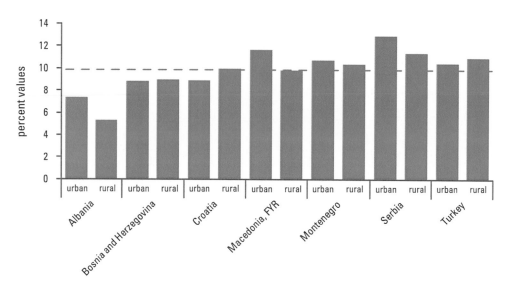

Sources: ECAPOV, World Bank estimates.

FIGURE 3.27

Energy Expenditure as a Share of Total Spending, Rural and Urban Areas, EPOC

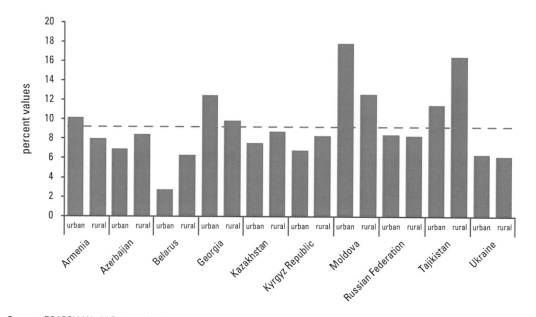

Sources: ECAPOV, World Bank estimates.

FIGURE 3.28

Comparison of Relative Electricity Tariff with Relative Electricity Consumption

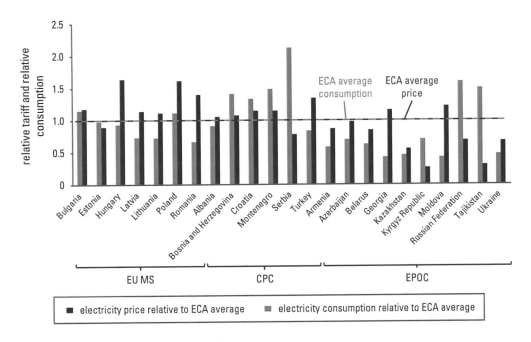

Sources: ECAPOV, World Bank estimates.

FIGURE 3.29

Comparison of Relative Gas Tariff with Relative Gas Consumption

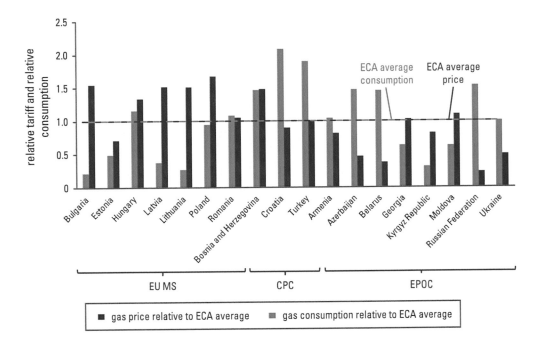

Sources: ECAPOV, World Bank estimates.

FIGURE 3.30

Main Categories of Household Spending as a Proportion of Total Household Expenditure

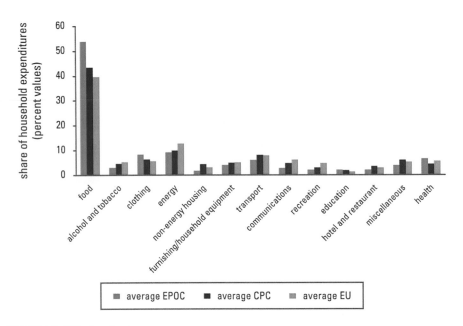

Sources: ECAPOV, World Bank estimates.

CHAPTER 4

Covering Costs and Coping
with Vulnerability

Given the differences in energy tariffs across the region, reaching a regional cost recovery standard would imply different price shocks for households in different countries. In most countries, the shock would be significant, resulting in increases in the energy budget share averaging 14 percent for EU MSs, 13 percent for the CPCs, and 28 percent for EPOC countries.[1] But there would be broad variations across these groupings. We do not find a general distributional pattern by which richer or poorer groups would be affected the most, but, even where poorer groups are not the most affected, poverty can increase significantly. Finally, the analysis of energy stress highlights how, in some countries, shocks to households are more uniformly distributed than in others, with possible implications for the political economy of the reforms.

Moving to Cost-recovery

Countries are situated differently in view of reaching the regional cost recovery standard of 12.5 U.S. cents/kWh for electricity (which rises to 16 U.S. cents/kWh for the EU-10 countries, to take into account environmental costs) and US$560/1,000 m^3 (that is, US$16.70/GJ) for gas that we have adopted for this report (figure 4.1).[2]

- In the EU-10, where almost all electricity household tariffs are above 10 U.S. cents/kWh (except for Bulgaria), the average price increase needed to reach cost recovery is expected to be about 38 percent.[3] For Bulgaria, it would reach 100 percent, while Hungary is already at the cost recovery level for electricity. Gas price increases would be on the same range, with Latvia, Lithuania, and Poland already at or close to cost recovery prices.

FIGURE 4.1

Estimated Average Price Increases Required to Move to Cost Recovery and Internalize Environmental Efficiency Costs

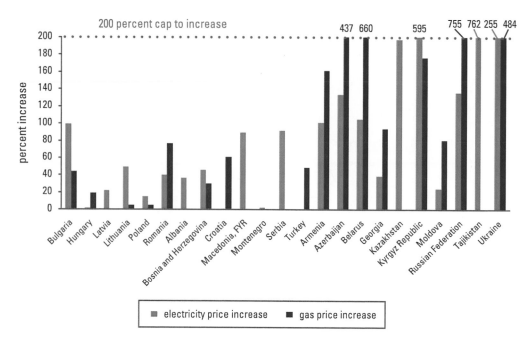

Sources: ECAPOV, World Bank estimates.

- In the CPCs, tariffs are in the range of 6.5 U.S. cents to 13.3 U.S. cents/ kWh and would require an average increase of 37 percent for residential electricity prices (Serbia would require a significantly higher increase, about 90 percent, while Montenegro is already at cost recovery levels). In addition to the electricity price increase, in Bosnia and Herzegovina and in Turkey, the gas price increase would be above 30 percent to reach cost recovery. (However, few households are supplied with gas in Bosnia and Herzegovina or in Turkey; see chapter 2.)

- In EPOC countries, except for Georgia and Moldova, electricity prices are far below cost recovery targeted prices and tariffs would need to increase significantly: by 235 percent for electricity prices (the Kyrgyz Republic and Tajikistan would require the highest electricity price increase) and by 356 percent for gas prices, on average (with Belarus and the Russian Federation requiring the highest gas price increases).[4] Only in Georgia and Moldova, where average residential prices are slightly above 10 U.S. cents/kWh for electricity and US$9/GJ for gas, the increase would remain limited to less than 100 percent for each energy source.

The increases in the energy budget share range widely across the region, from 12 percent in Tajikistan (if the increase is capped at 200 percent instead of 760 percent as required to reach the subregional average cost recovery level) to 51 percent in Armenia. The broad-brush picture that emerges from figure 4.2 is one of more moderate increases in EU MSs and more sustained ones in EPOC countries, with the CPC countries in an intermediate position. There is broad variation across these groupings. Among the EU MSs, Bulgaria and Romania would experience average increases of over 20 percent, while Serbia would register the highest increase (35 percent) among the CPCs. The EPOC countries would all experience average increases in the energy share between 12 and 50 percent, with the greatest increases in Armenia, Azerbaijan, and Belarus.

The magnitude of these increases is driven by the size of the tariff increase and the relative weight of electricity and gas in household energy spending. The countries with the greatest increase in energy shares are the CPCs and the EPOC countries, where the price increases are high and the initial energy shares are low. The countries with the greatest increases, Armenia (51 percent), Belarus (48 percent), Azerbaijan (41 percent), and Serbia (35 percent), would increase their electricity and gas prices by 104 and 187 percent, on average, for electricity and gas, respectively.[5] Kazakhstan and Tajikistan would not see such high increases in budget shares, despite increases in electricity tariffs of about 200 percent, because of the limited weight of electricity and gas in the budget shares.[6] Indeed, in both

FIGURE 4.2
Increase in Share of Household Expenditures on Energy

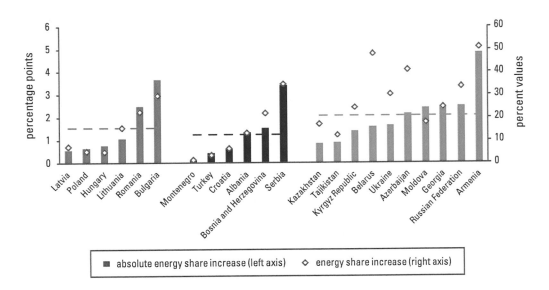

Sources: ECAPOV, World Bank estimates.

countries, the energy share would rise only by an estimated 16 and 12 percent, respectively.

Poverty Impacts

Figure 4.3 illustrates how this average impact would affect households in different quintiles. If one looks across the region, countries seem to be quite evenly split in terms of whether richer or poorer groups will experience the highest increases in the share of budgets needed to cover energy costs.

FIGURE 4.3
Increase in Energy Share of Total Household Expenditure, by Quintile of per Capita Expenditure

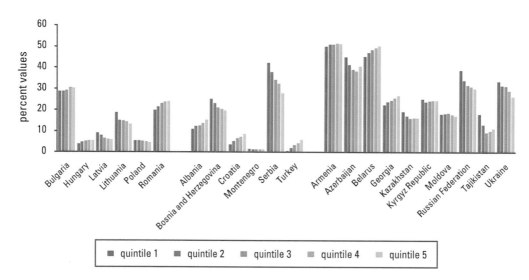

Sources: ECAPOV, World Bank estimates.

An alternative way of presenting the distributional impact (but one which gives a consistent picture) is through the welfare loss in terms of the consumer surplus due to the combined effect of increased expenditures and reduced consumption.[7] Figure 4.4 plots the welfare loss as a share of total expenditure, by quintile. The highest welfare losses are associated with the EPOC countries, where they exceed 3 percent of total expenditures, on average, for all households. In Armenia, Azerbaijan, and Russia, the losses are especially large. In about half the countries, the welfare losses are greatest for the poorest quintiles, and, in the remaining countries, with the exception of Moldova, Romania, and Turkey, the welfare losses are flat across the quintiles. Russia sees the steepest gradient, with the poorest quintile experiencing a welfare loss of 8.7 percent, and the wealthiest a welfare loss of only 2.3 percent.

FIGURE 4.4

Welfare Loss as a Share of Total Expenditures (Loss of Consumer Surplus)

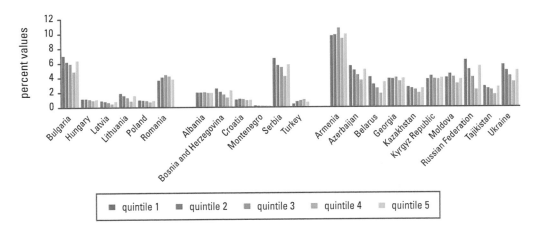

Sources: ECAPOV, World Bank estimates.

Electricity and gas price increases would raise poverty rates significantly in countries in which poverty incidence is low. Figure 4.5 contrasts existing levels of poverty incidence with the expected increases in poverty arising because of the tariff increase through a loss of purchasing power in household incomes. Even in EU MSs, where the simulated tariff increases are relatively minor, increasing tariffs to cost recovery could raise poverty incidence by between 5 and 30 percent. The largest increase

FIGURE 4.5

Poverty Incidence and Estimated Poverty Increase Because of the Tariff Increase

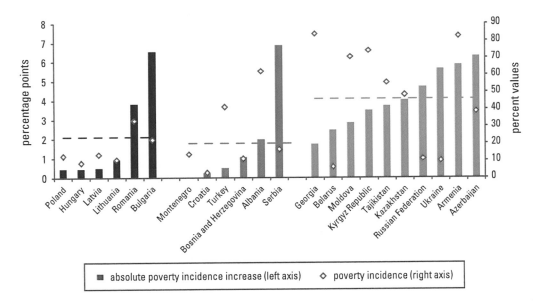

Sources: ECAPOV, World Bank estimates.

would be in Bulgaria, while Romania, the country with the highest poverty incidence in this group, would see an 11 percent increase, from 33 to 37 percent.

In the CPCs, the increase would occur in a range of 3 to 10 percent, except in Serbia, where the incidence of poverty would increase by 42 percent to reach 23 percent of the population (starting from 16 percent prior to the energy price increase).

In EPOC countries, the impact on poverty incidence is heterogeneous as is poverty incidence. In wealthier countries, such as Belarus, Russia, and Ukraine, where poverty incidence was low, the impact would be high. The highest increase in poverty incidence would occur in Ukraine (a 57 percent increase, from 10 to 16 percent), Russia (from 10 to 14 percent), and Belarus (by 50 percent, from 6 to 9 percent). The poverty rate in Azerbaijan would increase from 36 to 45 percent, and, in the rest of the EPOC countries, the already high poverty rates would increase from 4 to 8 percent.

Finally, figure 4.6 plots the impact of our simulated tariff increases on the incidence of energy poverty. The data show a negative correlation between the incidence of energy poverty before the price shock and the simulated increase. In general, countries in which more than half the population is already in energy poverty would not experience a high increase (for example, Hungary, Moldova, Poland, Tajikistan), while countries with low initial energy poverty incidence would experience high increases (for example, Azerbaijan and Ukraine). Bulgaria, Georgia, and Romania are exceptions to this pattern because, despite the high

FIGURE 4.6
Energy Poverty Incidence and Energy Poverty Increase

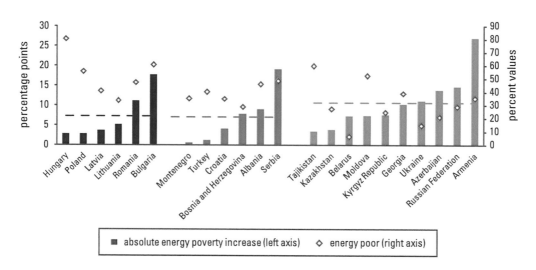

Sources: ECAPOV, World Bank estimates.

incidence, they would experience significant increases in energy poverty. Thus, energy poverty would increase from 61 to 78 percent in Bulgaria, from 47 to 59 percent in Poland, and from 39 to 49 percent in Georgia.

Given the pressures on household budgets captured by the notion of energy poverty, it is a particular concern if increases in energy poverty affect the poorest groups. In all countries but Serbia, our fixed elasticity simulations result in the largest increases in energy poverty among the more well off.[8]

As figure 4.7 shows, energy poverty among the less well off is particularly a concern in the EPOC countries, where several countries experience increases in energy poverty across the two poorest quintiles of at least 50 percent. Note that some of these increases are from a low base (for example, in Belarus, where energy poverty is less than 1 percent).[9]

FIGURE 4.7
Increase in Energy Poverty per Quintile of per Capita Expenditure

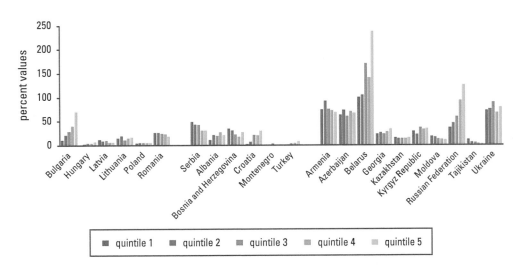

Sources: ECAPOV, World Bank estimates.

Absolute and Relative Energy Stress

Section B focuses on the poor and the energy poor because these groups are of particular policy relevance given their situation of need and the significant stress their household budgets would be under after large tariff increases. This section, in contrast, focuses on households that appear to be particularly affected by the increase, either in absolute or relative terms, because these are groups that, by standing to lose much from the reforms, have also the greatest interests in opposing them. This does not imply that all these groups would have to be compensated, but that the implementers of reform should be cognizant of whether particular groups are likely to be affected to a much greater extent than others.

For the purposes of this analysis, we introduce two separate measures of energy stress (figure 4.8). One is relative and focuses on households that have been affected significantly more than other households in a country (we adopt an increase in the energy share of 1.5 of the median increase as a threshold, though we have conducted sensitivity analyses based on twice the median increase as well). The other measure considers households that have been affected a lot, where "a lot" is measured in terms of whether the increase in spending exceeds the cost of 100kWh/month at preshock prices.[10]

FIGURE 4.8
Energy Stress Due to a Tariff Increase

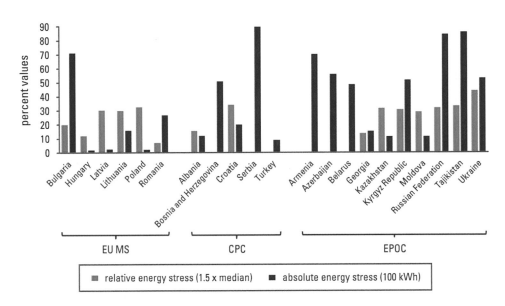

Sources: ECAPOV, World Bank estimates.

Absolute energy stress: As figure 4.8 shows, in all countries, with the exception of Montenegro, at least some households would be vulnerable in absolute terms. In many of them and particularly in the group of EPOC countries, at least 50 percent of households would be hit by a large shock. The share of vulnerable households ranges from 1.8 percent in Hungary to nearly 90 percent in Serbia. Because we simulate a price shock proportional to consumption, this measure of absolute energy stress captures households that were large consumers in contexts of large increases, especially if this is from a low base. The countries with the greatest rate of absolute energy stress, such as Armenia, Azerbaijan, the Kyrgyz Republic, Russia, Tajikistan, and Ukraine, all have the highest electricity and gas price increases.[11] Likewise, the relationship with consumption is clear. The countries with the highest household consumption of gas and electricity, on average, show higher absolute energy stress resulting from the energy price increase, such as Armenia, Belarus, Russia, and Ukraine.

Disaggregating absolute energy stress by quintile reveals that the poorest groups are least likely to be in this group, though, particularly in the EPOC countries with the highest predicted increases, the share of individuals in the bottom quintile who can be considered vulnerable in absolute terms is high.

Relative energy stress: The measurement of relative energy stress is based on the increase in the energy expenditure share of 1.5 times the median increase. As figure 4.8 shows, in some countries, the tariff adjustment results in more equitable impacts than in others; in Armenia, Azerbaijan, Bosnia and Herzegovina, Montenegro, Serbia, and Turkey, no households are deemed vulnerable according to our relative definition, as all increases are within 1.5 of the median. The impact on quintiles of the population also varies. In the countries with high rates of relative energy stress (over 30 percent, such as Croatia, Latvia, Lithuania, Poland, Russia, Tajikistan, and Ukraine), poorer groups seem to be most affected. In contrast, where relative energy stress is lower, the richest quintiles seem mostly affected.

Conclusions

Increasing energy costs will impact every household, rich or poor, because each has to dedicate more of the household budget to energy. This chapter and the simulations reveal great heterogeneity in the amounts by which prices will increase and in the impacts on economic levels across countries and regions.

Energy poverty increases after the price increases among every quintile in every group of countries; however, in some countries, the wealthiest quintile faces the highest increases. The bottom quintiles of the population often have energy poverty rates exceeding 60 percent in the EU and 40 percent in the Balkans and EPOC countries. In most cases, energy price increases will raise the share of households in energy poverty, but it will also even out the distribution of energy poverty among quintiles.

Energy stress measures show that all wealth quintiles may face significant shocks to their budgets. Relative energy stress measurements indicate that nonpoor households are as vulnerable as the poor households in about half the countries, with increases above 1.5 times the median price increase. Absolute energy stress, defined as an increase in energy expenditures above the cost of 100 kWh/month, reveals that the wealthiest quintile is the most vulnerable to energy price increases.

Endnotes

1. For the region as a whole, the increases in the energy share would range from the negligible (1 percent in Montenegro, where the expected electricity price increase is only 2 percent, or 5 percent in Poland, where the electricity price increase would reach 15 percent) to an estimated 51 percent (in Armenia, where the expected electricity price increase would reach 101 percent and the gas price 161 percent).
2. This is, of course, only an approximation of the country-specific cost recovery levels, which will vary by country depending on energy production technology and transmission systems.
3. We refer to pretax levels because there is relatively little variation in the taxation of energy sources across the region.
4. If the increase is capped at 200 percent, electricity prices in the EPOC countries would increase by 135 percent, and gas prices by 164 percent, on average.
5. The proportions of electricity and gas in Belarus energy expenditure are likely to be overestimated because part of these expenditures are in the housing aggregate and not taken into account in the total energy share (see the methodological annex).
6. Note that, in Tajikistan, only 6 percent of households are supplied with gas, but gas expenditures are totally missing in the survey.
7. The welfare loss captures the additional expenditure necessary to pay for the energy that the consumer continues to purchase at the higher price, plus the amount he would be willing to pay above the initial price for the quantity that is no longer purchased.
8. To the extent that our constant elasticity underestimates the options that richer groups might have of curtailing their consumption, our figures may be largely overestimated.
9. However, in Belarus, energy poverty is underestimated as district heating is not taken into account.
10. Because the shock is identified in terms of the cost of a given amount of electricity before the increase, the size of the shock might vary significantly across countries, but the idea is to capture the share of households which will receive monthly bills showing a significant increase.
11. Some countries with high consumption, such as Croatia and Hungary, have low absolute vulnerability rates because they experience only moderate increases.

CHAPTER 5

Towards Affordable Energy

As the impact of increasing household tariffs to reach cost recovery could significantly affect the livelihoods of large segments of the population in most countries in the region, there is a need for a more systematic policy solution to address the social cost of tariff increases. Some countries already have large programs to ensure energy affordability for parts of the population, though there is scope for increasing the effectiveness of these programs, particularly in a resource-constrained environment. The experience of the last decade points to new ways to improve the effectiveness of social assistance and help households manage demand more effectively. Both types of consideration need to be part of an integrated policy response: targeted social assistance measures should cater for the needs of the bottom end of the distribution, while incentives to increase efficiency should help all households to manage more effectively their demand. Particular attention should be given to phasing in the tariff increases with the effective capacity of existing measures to cushion the price shock and help households adapt. Temporary measures might be needed, while working to implement a longer-term strategy. As a set of ongoing case studies illustrate, specific policy recommendations need to be tailored to each country specificity to take into account the size of the expected price shock, the effectiveness of existing social assistance measures, and the needs in terms of improving demand management, given the status of the housing stock and infrastructure.

The Case for an Integrated Strategy

Faced with the prospect of price shocks that, in most countries, would significantly affect at least part of the population, the countries in Eastern Europe and Central Asia need to reconsider the policy solutions that they have put in place to ensure energy affordability for their populations.

These have involved some combination of tariff-based subsidies, which are aimed at smaller consumers as a proxy for poorer consumers (lifeline tariffs), and transfer programs, which are either earmarked for energy consumption or nonearmarked (box 5.1).

BOX 5.1
The Pros and Cons of Measures to Cushion the Impact of the Removal of Subsidies

A number of studies have analyzed the costs and benefits of the standard toolset to cushion the distributional impact of rising energy tariffs. Broadly, these studies highlight the following:

- Nonearmarked cash transfers (social assistance) have the potential to be the least distortionary of the utility subsidy mechanisms. If a social assistance system is already in place, the transfers can be implemented with no additional administrative requirements for the utility and will entail no financial burden for utilities or other (nonhousehold) consumers. Their effectiveness clearly depends on the targeting mechanism because they are often found to have an inadequate coverage among the poorest groups.

- Earmarked cash transfers (cash payments or vouchers to selected households for payment of a part of utility bills) can be handled by either the utility (as discounts) or by the social assistance system. In the former case, they tend to have a low net financial burden on utilities. In the latter case, they can be administratively difficult on both the demand and the supply side. They are generally accurate in directing benefits to the poor, but the coverage of the poor is highly uncertain and, in most countries, low.

- Lifeline tariffs—block tariffs designed so that the price for the bottom block of consumption is considerably lower than the average tariff (and production costs)—offer the benefit of high coverage of the poor if the poor are mostly connected. The leakage to the nonpoor is low in poorer countries and, in richer contexts, can be kept in check by defining the size of the initial block to cover only basic energy needs. Other advantages of these tariffs are that the benefits received are highly predictable, especially through a two-block lifeline tariff and that the scheme is simple to administer. In practice, leakage can be significant, and there is a significant burden on the budget (or on the finances of the utility or other consumers if the cost is recovered through a higher industrial tariff).

Sources: Lovei et al. 2000; Lampietti et al. 2007; Komives et al. 2005 ; UNDP 2011.

Lifeline tariffs have been an important plank of the policy advice provided by the Bank and others over the last decade given the ease of administration and the potential for high coverage of the poor in high-connection contexts such as is typically the case in the region. Experience in implementing these tariffs has been mixed (box 5.2), and their sustainability is now being questioned. The high costs to the budget and the leakage to nonpoor households that often characterize the tariff application in practice are illustrated by the Albania example in table 5.1. The subsidy embedded in the lifeline tariff is estimated to cover about 80

BOX 5.2
Mixed Results in Introducing Lifeline Tariffs over the Past Decade

In Moldova, an optional lifeline tariff was introduced in 2002, such that customers could opt into a scheme in which they were paying MLD 0.5 for the first 50 kWh of electricity and MLD 1.65 for consumption in excess of this threshold. However, as noted by Lampietti et al. (2007), only 10 percent of households enrolled, even though consumption levels were low, particularly among the poor. The authors suggest that one of the reasons may have been fears of high expenditures for exceeding the threshold.

In Hungary, there is some evidence that moving from a two- to a three-block tariff improved targeting. Estimates suggest that a three-block structure (0–50 kWh, 50–300 kWh, and 300+ kWh) priced such that the tariff for the first block was 17 percent below the price for the second block, and the tariff for the third block was 16 percent higher than that for the second block was generating a somewhat better targeting ratio than a two-block structure that omits the third block, while also resulting in a lower fiscal cost.

The experience of Serbia at the beginning of this decade suggests that "the introduction of the three-block tariff system created an incentive for households to use electricity efficiently (and in particular to reduce the consumption of electricity for heating), while keeping the price of non-heating electricity consumption within the financial reach of most households. Between the winters of 2000/2001 and 2001/2002, this enabled Electric Power Serbia to reduce heating demand successfully by 20 percent, while in the same period, according to household survey data, household expenditure on electricity was a relatively modest 4-6 percent of the household budget across all income deciles." (EBRD 2003, page 9).

In Albania, where the lifeline tariff for consumption of up to 300kWh was abolished in 2007 with the introduction of a flat tariff (block tariffs were then reintroduced in 2008), this resulted in a much higher impact on poor households than on nonpoor households. Waddams Price and Pham (2009) estimate that the effect on expenditures of the removal of the lifeline tariff on the bottom consumption quintile was four times the effect on the top quintile. This suggests that the lifeline tariff was providing needed support to poor households.

Sources: EBRD 2003; Lampietti 2007; Waddams Price and Pham 2009.

percent of the population and to be less progressive than the theoretical distribution of the social assistance program aimed at ensuring energy affordability. To the extent that lifeline tariff arrangements are based on a cross-subsidy by other consumers (industrial consumers or other, larger scale consumers), they are also against the EU acquis on energy.

As far as transfer programs are concerned, the majority of countries have put in place some form of energy-related social assistance program (ESA) to ensure energy affordability to some part of the population (annex 5.1). These programs vary under many profiles, according, for example, to the extent to which they are targeted to the poorest or categorical, probably two of the most relevant characteristics in terms of the program effectiveness in adequately reaching the poor (annex 5.2).

TABLE 5.1

Comparison of Targeting Performance: The Implicit Subsidy in the Tariff Structure and the Energy-Related Social Assistance Program, Albania 2008

Quintile	Performance of implicit subsidy through the tariff structure				Performance of energy program (simulated with eligibility criteria)			
	Coverage	Distribution of beneficiaries	Targeting	Generosity	Coverage	Distribution of beneficiaries	Targeting	Generosity
Q1	90.3	22.3	14.5	0.5	11.1	38.4	19.7	1.8
Q2	88.2	21.8	17.7	0.4	5.9	20.4	14.2	1.7
Q3	80.6	19.9	19.9	0.4	4.6	15.9	12.9	1.5
Q4	80.1	19.8	21.9	0.3	3.1	10.6	16.6	2.2
Q5	65.7	16.2	26.0	0.3	4.3	14.7	36.6	2.2
Total	**81.0**	**100**	**100**	**0.4**	**5.8**	**100**	**100**	**1.9**

Source: World Bank 2011b.

Comparing the coverage, targeting performance, and generosity of the programs shows that social assistance programs that are means-tested typically have higher targeting, but lower coverage. Categorically targeted programs generally have much higher coverage, especially if a list of eligible groups is extensive, but they often lack in targeting, because eligibility status is not connected with income. These programs would also perform poorly in a post-increase scenario, considering a number of potential target groups that might be seen as deserving of protection (box 5.3). This suggests that significant resources would have to be invested in ESAs to increase their coverage of the targeted groups.

As current data on ESAs show, however, high coverage and generosity do not come cheap; for example, nominative compensations in Moldova, which have the highest levels of coverage in the region and are also generous, entail significant budgetary cost (in 2008, they accounted for 0.5 percent of GDP in Moldova, or 30 percent of total social assistance spending) since more than two thirds of all spending on nominative compensations goes to the nonpoor.[1] As a result, as discussed below, the government of Moldova recently froze the existing program and introduced a new one.

The tradeoff between the greater coverage of the poorest and the costs of the programs that characterizes ESAs characterizes more broadly the set of choices that countries have. Lifeline tariffs, which offer the benefits of high coverage, end up leaking significant amounts of benefits to nonpoor groups. This would be exacerbated in a context of growing energy prices. ESAs, on the other hand, particularly targeted programs that offer the benefit of limiting fiscal spending, cover a low proportion of the poor.

BOX 5.3
How Would Existing ESAs Perform in Reaching the Groups Most Affected by a Move to Cost Recovery in Household Tariffs?

How well would existing ESA perform in reaching those most affected by future tariff increases? We have investigated the question with some simple simulations. Note that some of the ESAs might increase their coverage by design after a tariff increase, but we focus here on their current distribution to have a sense of how much larger they would need to be to cater to the needs of those most affected. Given data limitation, this exercise has been conducted only on 4 countries: figure 5.1 below shows the findings in terms of coverage of those who would be poor after the shock, as well as other groups. Looking across the groups targeted it seems that the best coverage on average would be the one of those who are in the bottom 40 percent and are vulnerable in relative terms. Even looking at the case for which coverage is highest (the bottom 40 percent and the absolutely vulnerable in the case of Moldova) coverage remains however relatively low.

FIGURE 5.1
ESA Coverage of Households both at the Bottom of the Distribution and Severely Affected by the Energy Tariff Shock

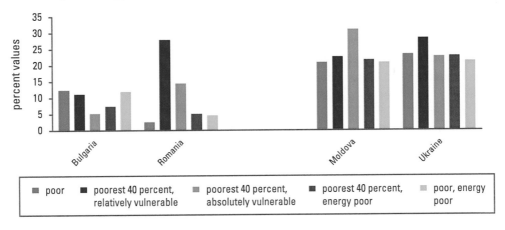

Sources: ECAPOV, World Bank estimates.

This is partly intended, partly the byproduct of design features, including the ease of applying for the program, the way the program design is implemented, and budget constraints, which, at least in certain countries, limit the effective coverage of these programs (box 5.4).

Helping households cope and adjust according to the type of shocks described in the previous chapter calls for an integrated strategy centered on three main pillars, as discussed in the rest of this chapter, as follows:

- continuing reforms to ensure that social assistance in general and energy-related social assistance in particular are more effective at reaching the poorest;

BOX 5.4
Low Take-up of Energy Programs: Insights from Focus Groups in Serbia and Albania

The current programs to support energy affordability for vulnerable groups in Serbia are small. The program targeted at LRSA recipients covers about 0.5 percent of metered households (based on the first three months of 2010), while the program for other households in extreme social need covers 0.7 percent of metered households. As a comparison, a general discount offered to households that pay their bills within two weeks of receiving the bill covers approximately 40 percent of metered households, and the recent decision not to extend the latest increase in tariffs to the first consumption block sheltered 32 percent of households in which consumption is exclusively in that block (71 percent of which are not in the bottom quintile). Evidence from focus groups provides some context to this low coverage. The conditionality on paying the bills appears to be a major obstacle to claiming the benefit, particularly as poor people stop paying their bills even partially if the interest accumulated is too high and if mechanisms to renegotiate payments appear to require a down payment that, for them, is too high to be a real option. Low generosity of the benefits, together with cumbersome procedures (and, for some respondents, the stigma of applying for the benefit at the LRSA office), combine to decrease the incentives to apply for these benefits.

Similar insights have emerged in Albania, where the energy benefit scheme is similarly small. Focus groups show that households that are already recipients of LRSA, which, in itself, is quite cumbersome, are in favor of the addition of more energy benefits as a top up, while other poor beneficiaries are against this approach. Note that the coverage of LRSA is quite small, and, even if the program is currently being reformed to enhance the transparency of the process and reduce the discretion of local offices, the application procedures can be a serious barrier to accessing the benefits.

Sources: IPSOS 2011; IDRA 2011.

- integrating demand management policies in the strategy to help households deal with the tariff shock; and

- ensuring a smooth transition, while these measures are put in place.

Such an integrated package is not going to come cheap, but, as discussed in the next and final chapter, it is feasible.

Improving the Effectiveness of Social Assistance

Over the last few years, but particularly since the beginning of the crisis in 2008, a number of countries have introduced important reforms in social assistance systems to increase effectiveness at a time of growing needs and tight budgets. Many of these affect also the design of ESAs. Efforts have been made, for example, to strengthen the targeting of the programs, moving away from some of the categorical benefits. Recent changes in the eligibility criteria for district heating subsidies in Romania for example (box 5.5) were introduced to ensure that the program could better cushion the impact of the removal of central subsidies for district heating producers. In addition, some of the filters added to the means-tested or proxy means-tested programs have been revised so as to diminish the disincentives to work and to remove some of the exclusionary barriers toward the working poor. Finally, efforts have been put in place to create more transparent and accountable systems, which might also cut down on the bureaucratic requirements that can make applying for the benefits burdensome for potential beneficiaries. These efforts are seeking to create a unified registry of beneficiaries and consolidate the plurality of small programs that characterize the overall social assistance system.

BOX 5.5
Using Poverty and Social Impact Analysis to strengthen the design of ESAs in Romania

The Romanian Government removed district heating (DH) subsidies in 2011 to meet its EU commitments and to improve its fiscal position. The DH system covers about one fifth of the population, and is concentrated in one third of the largest cities. In terms of per capita income, 42 percent of DH users belong to the richest quintile, and another 37 percent to the second highest income quintile.

Given the high rate of subsidization, the removal of central heating subsidies could have had a major impact on consumer welfare. The removal of central subsidies to producers could have increased charges by up to 45 percent on average. If in addition producer subsidies from local budgets were also removed, the DH prices would have increased by as much as 86 percent on average, and up to 300-400 percent in some cities. To protect vulnerable groups from such cost increases, the Government aimed to expand the Heating Benefit program relying on means-tested allocations.

A poverty and social impact analysis (PSIA), conducted by the Ministry of Labor, Family and Social Protection and the World Bank, explored cost-efficient solutions to mitigate the impact of the subsidy removal. A number of parametric reforms were tested to preserve affordability for low-and middle-income households, generate fiscal savings, create a framework for local government to shift from producer subsidies to complementary heating benefit support, and to ensure adequate political support for reform. The PSIA simulations were based on micro data from the Household Budget Survey (HBS) and calibrated to administrative data. They compared the cost and distributional performance of two types of benefit formulae: one using the concept of "energy poverty", another based on compensation of the increased DH bill. The "energy poverty" formula compensates the heating costs above a certain income threshold. The second preserved the status quo but expanded the coverage of the program: households are compensated for a share of the heating bill, based on their per capita income and household size. The simulations tested a number of program parameters for each of the alternatives including: the cost of the program, the expected number of beneficiaries, the estimated impact of the program on poverty, and the distributional impact of the benefits.

The simulations showed that a program aimed at reducing energy poverty would eliminate the occurrence of high shares of heating costs relative to the household incomes but would not ensure horizontal equity. In addition such an alternative would provide perverse incentives for overconsumption. The alternative which compensates for part of the heating cost would cover a larger share of the population, had a lower fiscal cost and allowed better targeting. In addition, by preserving the parameters of the DH program used in the past, this alternative minimized the risk of error or fraud as both the front line staff and the population already know the rules. For these reasons, the Government selected the second alternative, and the new law that came into force in August 2011.

FIGURE 5.2
Total fiscal costs of different reform scenarios

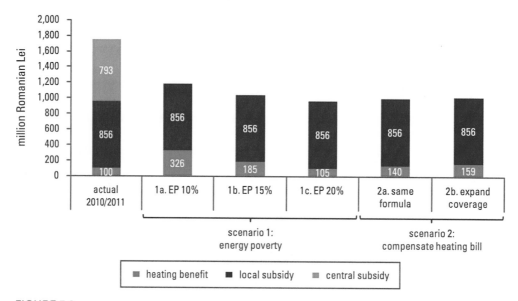

FIGURE 5.3
Targeting of heating benefits under different reform scenarios

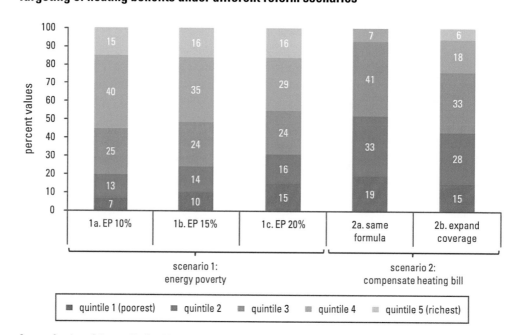

Source: Corches, Grigoras, Tesliuc 2012.

To the extent that these reforms strengthen targeting, they may contribute to making ESAs more effective. Simple simulations on the effects of reallocating the current ESA budgets on either the bottom quintile or the current beneficiaries of LRSA (box 5.6) show that improving targeting can lead to significant improvements in terms of energy poverty.[2] In EU MSs, where targeting is stronger, the improvements would be more limited. Note, however, that the scale of the programs is often too small to make a big dent in energy poverty so that increasing generosity and ensuring a fuller coverage of the most needy should be part of the reform.

Part of the consolidation efforts of social assistance programs has been the tightening of links between means tested programs and energy programs. Such links can take different forms: in countries where there are already well developed registries, it is possible to make the beneficiary of last resort eligible for special subsidies administered by either the utility (as in Poland) or by the social assistance system. As an alternative, pro-

---

BOX 5.6
Simulated Impacts of Reallocating ESA Budgets toward the Poorest or the LRSA Recipients

Simulation 1 shows the impact of targeting the existing budget toward all households in quintile 1. We assume a uniform allocation. This type of reform would have the largest impact where significant resources are being spent because the program is generous or where the coverage is large, such as in the case of Moldova and Ukraine. In other countries, the absolute and relative impact of these measures would be more limited (figures 5.4 and 5.5), particularly in EU MSs, where the targeting of resources is already quite strong.

FIGURE 5.4
Simulation 1: Change in Energy Poverty (Absolute Change)

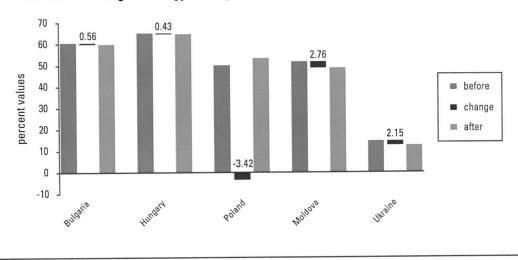

FIGURE 5.5
Simulation 2 (LRSA): Change in Energy Poverty (Absolute Change)

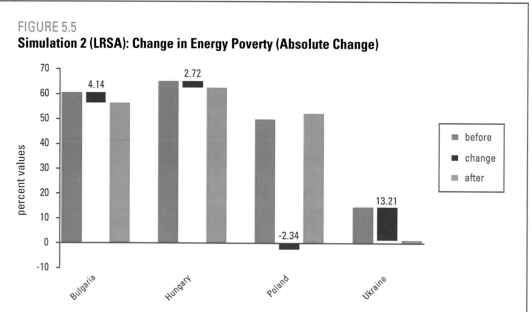

Simulation 2 in figure 5.5 shows the impacts of strengthening the links between ESAs and targeted programs by targeting ESAs to LRSA-recipient households, a group that is generally smaller than the group receiving energy benefits. In the case of Ukraine, for example, over 20 percent of households receive the energy benefit, and about 12 percent receive the LRSA.

While more effectively targeting resources currently channeled through ESA by strengthening their links to other targeted programs would reduce energy poverty, the need for significantly extending targeted remains. Figure 5.6 shows how well current LRSA programs cover different groups that could potentially be targeted for support after a price shock. While the performance varies by country and target group, it is no more than 15 percent of the target in most cases.

FIGURE 5.6
Coverage of Poor Households by Existing LRSA Programs

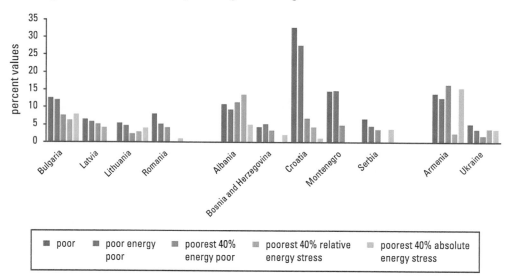

Sources: ECAPOV, World Bank estimates.

grams have been set up based on a common targeting scheme (means testing or proxy means testing), but higher thresholds to define eligibility for the energy subsidy have also been put in place. An interesting example of the latter is Moldova (box 5.7), where communicating clearly that different needs are being taken into account within a common delivery mechanism has been an important part of the process of moving to a consolidated social assistance system.

BOX 5.7
Strengthening Safety Nets and Energy Programs in Moldova

To improve the effectiveness of the safety nets in general, including of energy programs, the Moldovan government created a two-way track. It froze the categorical nominative compensation program to new entrants and the value of its benefit levels, while introducing a new means tested program (Adjutor Social) that included a new targeted heating allowance program for a few months of the year.

The new energy program was first focused on recipients of LRSA only and then, more recently, expanded to cover those within the 1.5 band of the minimum income threshold guaranteed by the LRSA. The transition between the two schemes will be facilitated by the fact that almost 40 percent of the beneficiaries of the first scheme are eligible also for the second scheme. An important element that needs to be managed in the transition toward more consolidated means tested programs remains the visibility of the earmarked programs. The existence of two notionally separate benefits linked to the same targeting system is seen as an important element of the communication around this new program to make it clear that policy responses are being taken as part of the transition to higher tariffs. Managing the transition between systems through appropriate temporary arrangements and communicating clearly the nature of the changes are two important elements that recent reform experience suggests increase the political buy-in in these reforms, while mitigating the social impact of higher energy tariffs.

Source: World Bank 2011a.

It is worth drawing attention to the adoption of a different eligibility threshold in Moldova as the adoption of a unified system for, say, LRSA and ESA is not necessarily without problems. Where filters based on ownership are applied for targeted programs, for example, the programs might end up excluding groups such as the urban poor who might own their apartments and still find themselves hard pressed to face higher energy bills due to the characteristics of their housing, as discussed in the previous section. Adopting higher thresholds or not applying some of the filters might be one solution to this problem, though the specifics of the vulnerability profile and of the targeting system would need to be addressed on a country-specific basis.

A less systemic, but equally important development seen in the last few years is the recourse to easy-to-implement and often flat payment schemes either on a temporary or on a regular basis. An example of a temporary scheme includes a three-month flat payment that is distributed to selected vulnerable categories in Moldova before the new program starts covering them. An example of the regular scheme is the flat payment top-up of LRSA adopted in FYR Macedonia, which is the object of an ongoing evaluation. What these experiences have in common is the need to identify a quick disbursing measure to address times of stress, without creating a new entitlement for recipients that would require more careful design and consideration. Note also that the introduction of flat payments and, more generally, the delinking of the benefit from either energy consumption or budget shares are an important development and could help support increased energy efficiency also by poor groups. This type of measure, while often not first-best, reveals a serious concern about reaching vulnerable groups, while working on setting up more complex, state of the art means tested programs. While little attention has been given to this type of arrangement in the past, more attention should be given to understanding and evaluating properly these measures to identify best practice even in setting up this type of temporary arrangement.

Finally, while most of these innovations have occurred in government programs, private sector operators have also tried to find new ways to work in poor communities to increase the enforcement of bill payments and address the issue of debt on past bills.[3] The example of the Roma community of Plodviv (box 5.8) offers insights on how a tailored approach to a given local community might end up creating mutual benefits.

BOX 5.8
A Private Sector Solution to Service in Poor Communities

EVN, an Austrian company active in Bulgaria since 2005 in the supply and distribution of electricity, has piloted a new approach to service in a poor community, starting in the predominantly Roma community of Stolipinovo (Plovdiv).

Faced with 3 percent collection rates, dilapidated infrastructure, and about a third of facilities without connection, EVN upgraded the infrastructure and installed a distant reading system and remote controls on electricity consumption. These measures, which were aimed at enforcing payment and reducing technical losses, were coupled with a process of mediation with the local communities. As part of the agreement, the €6 million of unpaid debt accumulated in this community of about 50,000 people was largely condoned. Regular communication with a group of representatives to address emerging issues (problems with equipment and suspicions about high bills due to a particular cold winter) was also established, and so was a partnership with NGOs that would finance the costs of connection for unserved households. This approach saw an increase in collection rates to over 80 percent and a reduction of technical losses from 40 to 8 percent. The approach has been replicated in many other communities in the country.

Source: EVN 2008.

Helping Households Manage

In Eastern Europe and Central Asia, energy intensity, which largely depends on the structure of the economy, remains high, and efficiency in power generation and consumption is low. Most of the efficiency potential is on the demand side, but to decrease energy intensity (or increasing output per unit of energy input) requires more than simply adjusting prices to reflect the cost of supply. Incentivizing consumers to reduce demand is equally important. This includes developing energy efficiency strategies and implementing energy efficiency programs, disseminating information to assist users, comprehensive planning to address all issues, offering grants and funds, developing and updating building standards, and helping owners and renters implement energy efficiency measures in buildings. Finally, although changes in laws and regulations can be undertaken quickly, changes in behavior are notoriously slow. Specific

---

BOX 5.9

Better Informed Choices for Consumers: Managing Peak-Time Demand and Certificate Programs

Supplying energy requires having the installed capacity to meet demand at peak hours, typically provided at higher marginal costs. Inducing households and industry to lower consumption at peak hours reduces the need for peak-load capacity. Variable pricing and customer awareness are the key tools. Households pay annualized electricity tariffs, thus paying more than the cost of generation during low demand hours (for example, at night) and paying less than the cost of generation during peak hours (such as at midday in the summer). Time-of-use pricing, also known as dynamic pricing, involves charging different rates throughout time periods each day, more closely following the actual marginal cost of generation, with the intention of shifting some energy consumption to smooth demand. To implement time-of-use pricing, utilities and households must install smart meters, which represent an expensive investment. A solution that is easier to implement relies on educating users about reducing electricity consumption at peak hours.

Certificate programs are an additional innovative tool to provide incentives for increased energy efficiency. A white certificate program has been implemented in the France, Italy, the United Kingdom, and, more recently, Australia. Governments or regulators establish specific time-bound energy savings targets for energy suppliers or distributors, who must meet the targets by implementing energy efficiency measures among their clients. Energy suppliers or distributors who exceed their targets can sell their unused white certificates to suppliers and distributors who have fallen short of their targets. Alternatively, they can buy white certificates against a substitute or penalty fee from the regulator. Simpler schemes eliminate the certificate trading component and merely impose energy savings obligations on energy suppliers or distributors. These programs have proven successful. They have all exceeded their initial multiyear energy savings targets and achieved cost savings on the order of 0.5–2.0 € cents/kWh, including direct and indirect costs.

Source: World Bank 2012a.

measures such as introducing smart metering and certificate programs can help because they allow households to take informed decisions (box 5.9). Compared with these comprehensive efforts, promoting improvements is easier on the supply side, where there are relatively few large power producers instead of millions of end users.

Based on the data available for a subset of EU MSs, the trend of the last decade has been rather mixed (figures 5.7 and 5.8). While there have been improvements in the use of energy for heating, consumption of electricity has gone up in some countries. Indeed, electricity consumption has gone up in the EU as a whole as a reflection of how improved living standards have multiplied the number of electrical appliances households use. This makes the goal of improving energy efficiency a moving target.

A parallel report (World Bank 2012a) investigates how to scale up investments in this area and accelerate the decline in energy intensities among households and across economic sectors. The report reviews the effectiveness of policies, programs, and projects that have been used in the region and selectively analyzes why specific approaches have failed to meet expectations. For instance, partial credit guarantees aim to reduce the risk carried by private sector lenders who may lack the experience to evaluate the viability of energy efficiency projects. These guarantees have been instrumental in scaling up building efficiency improvements in energy in Hungary, but have failed in several other countries. Other insights on what works in practice to increase energy efficiency in lower-income contexts have been provided by a recent report by the World Energy Council (box 5.10).

Smoothing the Transition to Efficiency with Equity

Adopting this new comprehensive approach to help households adapt and cope with higher energy tariffs will require time. Countries in the region are positioned differently in terms of social assistance systems and the introduction of measures to provide incentives for energy efficiency. In particular, not all countries have targeted social assistance programs in place that are capable of ensuring appropriate coverage at the lower end of the distribution, and those that have good targeted programs might still need to extend the coverage to make the programs more effective policy tools. Moreover, measures such as setting up a unified registry and connecting all social assistance offices to a common system, or devising, piloting, and adopting new targeting criteria are not tasks that can be completed rapidly. Similarly, demand management measures, once the easy gains have been achieved, might require significant, protracted investment.

FIGURE 5.7
Change in Consumption per Dwelling for Lighting and Electric Appliances, 2000–09

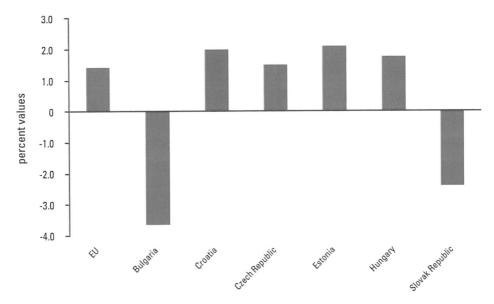

Source: ODYSSEE database.

FIGURE 5.8
Change in Consumption per Dwelling for Space Heating, 2000–09

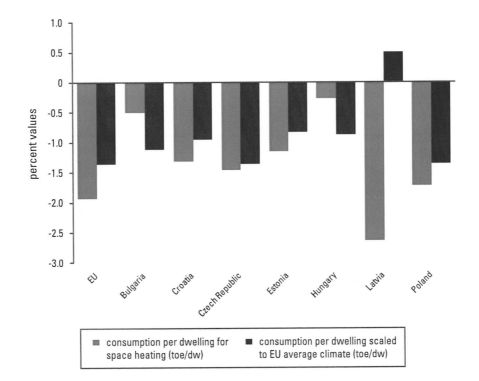

Source: ODYSSEE database.

BOX 5.10
What Works in Improving Energy Efficiency in Low-Income Contexts

The World Energy Council conducted a study of energy efficiency policies and measures targeted on low-income households. Generally, energy efficiency programs work as secondary or complementary tools to decrease the rate of poverty or energy poverty or to protect vulnerable households. Energy efficiency programs reduce the cost of primary measures, such as direct financial transfers, and the number of energy efficiency programs has increased in recent years.

The World Energy Council assessed four public initiatives in Brazil, South Africa, the United Kingdom, and the United States. Public initiatives are the most common programs because energy efficiency measures require significant funding. As with direct financial assistance, the difficulty in energy efficiency programs for low-income/energy poor households is defining eligibility criteria to minimize leakage to nontarget households, while also minimizing administrative costs. Implementation is often devolved at the local level by local authorities, associations, and nongovernmental organizations, to reach the targeted households, or through public-private partnerships. Another key factor is having a sufficiently skilled and numerous workforce to provide inspections, surveys, audits, and deployment of energy efficiency tools.

The World Energy Council found that the most effective energy efficiency programs for low-income or energy poor households were:

• develop effective targeting to maximize assistance, while minimizing leakage, and develop specific approaches with local partnerships
• find the correct funding level to make energy efficiency actions affordable for vulnerable households, but also sufficiently moderate costs so that it is possible to offer support to the highest number of households
• establish a broad list of eligible items to avoid the unfair distribution of assistance
• undertake regular monitoring and evaluation to allow continuous improvement
• support peripheral activities, such as training schemes, that allow large-scale change through energy efficiency programs

Source: World Energy Council 2010.

Transitional measures might therefore be needed to start reaping the benefits of greater efficiency, while the country moves toward implementing this agenda. The scope for transitional measures varies widely across countries and can operate at many levels, from calibrating payment modalities to match household needs more closely to revising the subsidy structure, to the introduction of temporary social assistance measures.

• Calibrating payment modalities to match household needs: as an example of these measures consider that in countries in which noncollection has subsidized consumers for a long time, stricter enforcement of payment could be accompanied by an effort to ensure that households can afford to renegotiate their arrears and to link this explicitly to improvements in the quality of service. Similarly, the introduction of payment modalities that allow households to smooth their energy bills throughout the year and therefore avoid falling into arrears during the months when more energy is needed for heating could remove some of the stress that households face.

- Revising the subsidy structure: examples of this second type of intervention include the introduction of seasonally adjusted tariffs that would maintain the subsidy, but only during the coldest months of the year, or adjustments in the lifeline tariffs such as a decrease in the size of the first block or the recalibration of the whole tariff structure to ensure that the costs of energy are covered even if the first block remains subsidized. This last type of intervention might be effective especially in the poorer countries in the region, where leakages to the nonpoor are more limited and where, despite low tariffs, energy poverty is already high. Similar transitional measures might apply also in countries that do have delivery systems for social assistance, but with limited coverage, such as in the case of some CPCs. The extent to which the measures can be effectively implemented, though, might be limited by elements of the EU *acquis communautaire* (or the way elements of the EU acquis have been translated into national legislation): this applies in particular to limits to cross-subsidization across different consumer groups, which can eliminate the possibility of adapting lifeline tariffs.

- Temporary social assistance measures: some countries have introduced temporary or ad hoc measures to cushion the impact of price increases, while working on longer-term solutions. Flat payments, or vouchers, for example, can be helpful in increasing the reach of exiting transfer schemes during the transition to a new system while preserving incentives to limit energy consumption. These programs should not create new entitlements that would have to be revoked later. Gradual adjustments to the targeting mechanisms of different programs, whereby the coverage of existing energy benefits is expanded by making some of the eligibility filters less binding could also be considered in this category of temporary adjustments.

The way tariff increases are managed might also help during the transition. While, over the 1990s, there were experiences involving sharp shocks with sudden major increases in prices, this option is no longer on the table, particularly in the context of the current crisis. A steady pace of increases toward a given cost recovery rate would give households more time and opportunities to adjust consumption levels, particularly if simpler measures to ensure better demand management, such as incentives to buy energy efficient appliances, are already in place.

Conclusions

The impact of removing energy subsidies for households, particularly in a rising price context, is such that countries need to put in place integrated systems of measures that provide support to the poorer groups, while offering incentives for all households to manage demand more effectively.

Most countries already have some ESA measures in place, but many of these programs are too small to serve the targeted groups effectively. EU MSs in the region tend to have more well targeted means-tested ESAs. Continuing the efforts ongoing in many countries to increase the coverage of ESAs within the context of creating more transparent and accountable systems and consolidating targeted benefits represent an opportunity for increasing the effectiveness of these measures.

A second pillar of this integrated strategy will involve scaling up existing successful examples of efforts to reduce residential energy demand. While a number of easy-to-achieve opportunities might be available, addressing these issues comprehensively might require longer-term investments. Because it would be fiscally unsustainable to compensate large parts of the population, however, these measures will be essential to help middle-class households adapt to a higher energy price environment.

Finally, because putting in place effective measures to help households adapt and cope with higher energy tariffs is going to require time, countries should assess the temporary or transitional measures that might be needed to avoid sharp shocks with which households would have difficulty coping.

Endnotes

1. Nominative compensations cover both energy utility bills (heating, natural gas, electricity, liquid gas in cylinders, coal, and firewood) and other utilities (cold and hot water consumption, sewerage). Our analysis does not discriminate between these different items; so, it might be overestimating the generosity of the benefits in a comparative perspective. For the 2008 data, see World Bank (2011a).

2. These simulations do not account for the cost for households that will lose their housing benefit, often groups in specific categories, such as veterans, the disabled, and so on, though we briefly discuss the political economy considerations of pursuing a policy change of this nature. The simulations are also limited to first order effects, assuming that absolute household en-

ergy consumption remains fixed following a change incomes. Finally, we take as a given the targeting of the existing last resort programs. In each simulation, we simulate the impact on energy poverty (defined as the percentage of households that allocate more than 10 percent of their spending on energy) and on the energy share (defined as the percentage of household spending allocated to energy, for the average household).

3. Because new technology allows utility companies to enforce payments more effectively than they did in the past, nonpayment and illegal connections, two widespread coping strategies in poor settings, are going to be increasingly difficult to adopt for poor households, thereby emphasizing the need to find ways to ensure energy affordability.

References

Corches, Grigoras, Tesliuc 2012 - Staying Warm in a Cold Fiscal Climate: How the Government of Romania used PSIA to reform its heating subsidies, World Bank unpublished report

EBRD (European Bank for Reconstruction and Development). 2003. "Can the Poor Pay for Power? The Affordability of Electricity in South East Europe". London: EBRD.

EVN, 2008. "'Stolipinovo, Bulgaria': A European Case Study."

IDRA Research and Consulting (2011) "Impact of Energy Reforms on Vulnerable Households".

IPSOS Strategic Marketing. 2011. "Poor People Energy Use Patterns and Strategies to Cope with Tariff Increases.

Komives, K., V. Foster, J. Halpern, and Q. Wodon. 2005. "Water, Electricity and the Poor: Who Benefits from Utility Subsidies?" World Bank, Washington, DC.

Lampietti, J. A. 2007. "People and Power: Electricity Sector Reforms and the Poor in Europe and Central Asia." World Bank, Washington, DC.

Lovei, L., E. Gurenko, M. Haney, P. O'Keefe, and M. Shkaratan. 2000. "Maintaining Utility Services for the Poor -- Policies and Practices in Central and Eastern Europe and the Former Soviet Union."

UNDP (United Nations Development Programme). 2011. "Energy and Communal Services in Kyrgyzstan and Tajikistan: A Poverty and Social Impact Assessment." UNDP Bratislava Regional Centre, Bratislava.

Waddams Price, C. and K. Pham. 2009. "The Impact of Electricity Market Reform on Consumers", Utilities Policy 17: 1

World Bank. 2000. "Maintaining Utility Services for the Poor: Policies and Practices in Central and Eastern Europe and the Former Soviet Union." World Bank, Washington, DC.

———. 2009 "Bulgaria: Social Assistance Programs: Cost, Coverage, Targeting and Poverty Impact. World Bank, Washington, DC.

————. 2010 a. "Lights Out: The Outlook for Energy and Eastern Europe and Central Asia." World Bank, Washington, DC.

————. 2010 b. "Tajikistan: Delivering Social Assistance to the Poorest Households". Report No.: 56593-TJ.

————. 2011a. Moldova - Strengthening the Effectiveness of the Social Safety Net Project" Project Appraisal Document, World Bank, Washington, DC.

————. 2011b. "Electricity Tariffs and Protection of Vulnerable Households in Albania. Unpublished report, World Bank, Washington, DC.

————. 2012a. "Energy Efficiency in ECA-- Lessons Learned from Success Stories." World Bank, Washington, DC.

World Energy Council. 2010. "Measures Focused on Low-Income Households." WEC-ADEME Case Studies on Energy Efficiency Measures and Policies.

Housing and Heating Benefits in Eastern Europe and Central Asia

Country	Benefit	Description/eligibility
Albania	Electricity subsidy	The electricity subsidy program, implemented in 2003, provides additional support to *Ndihma Ekonomike* (LRSA) beneficiaries. It is meant to compensate them for the increase in energy prices. The program provides eligible households with a lump sum subsidy of lek 640, equivalent to a subsidy of lek 3.2 for the first 200 kWh consumed.
Armenia	Gas subsidy	Since 2010 the Family Benefit (FB) has been increased to help beneficiaries pay for gas. In 2010 this was done through a 15 percent increase in the benefits. In 2011 those registered in the FB database (i.e. those who have applied, whether or not they meet the eligibility criteria) received a 30 percent discount on 300 cubic meter of gas. In 2012 the discount was limited for FB recipients only.
Bulgaria	Heating benefit	Persons and families whose income is lower than the differentiated minimum income for heating have the right to a targeted heating allowance. The differentiated minimum income for heating is determined as a percentage of the guaranteed minimum income and varies from 183.6 to 288.0 percent according to the category of individuals in the same way as the differentiated minimum income for monthly social assistance (guaranteed minimum income) allowances, except that the percentages involved for heating are slightly higher.
Bulgaria	Housing benefit	Individuals whose income for the preceding month is less than 150 percent of the differentiated minimum income have a right to a targeted monthly allowance for payment of rents for municipality lodgings. The allowance is granted to orphans up to the age of 25, lone elderly people over the age of 70, and single parents.
Kazakhstan	Housing assistance	Housing assistance is compensation to low-income and vulnerable groups to cover expenses for housing maintenance, utilities, and leasing of housing. Housing assistance is extended to poor households if their actual housing and utilities expenses exceed a certain percentage of the aggregate household income defined by the local government. Local authorities define the size of and procedure for obtaining housing assistance, as well as eligibility (the size is determined by local executive bodies and varies from 10 to 25 percent). Local budgets fund the assistance.

Country	Benefit	Description/eligibility
Kyrgyz Republic	Categorical *lgoti*	The largest group of privileges beneficiaries—families living in mountainous regions—is entitled to a specific electricity subsidy. Eligibility is mainly categorical and independent of household income.
Latvia	Housing benefit	The amount of the benefit varies by municipality depending on the available resources. If a person is granted the status of a needy person and has expressed a wish to be a tenant of a social flat (public housing), the person can rent a flat as social housing in which reduced rent and utility payments are charged.
Lithuania	Reimbursement for the cost of house heating and hot and cold running water	The benefit is provided for low-income families and based on a means test. A family should not have to pay more than 20 percent of the family income above the guaranteed minimum income (state-supported income, that is, LTL 350 or €101 per family member to heat a standard size accommodation; 5 percent of the family income for a basic standard of hot water; 2 percent of the family income for a basic standard of cold water. The standard size of accommodation is defined as 38 square meters for 1 person, and 12 square meters for each additional person living with them.
Moldova	Nominative compensations (housing and utilities compensations)	Nominative compensations are cash benefits paid on categorical principles from the state budget to support the payment of heating bills, hot and cold water consumption, natural gas consumption, sewerage, electricity bills, liquid gas in cylinders, coal, and firewood consumption. These allowances are calculated based on the nominative cost and monthly energy consumption. They compensate between 25 to 50 percent of the utilities bill or the acquisition of coal and firewood depending on the category of beneficiary. In 2010, new beneficiaries were no longer accepted. A new means-tested program was introduced in 2011.
Hungary	Home maintenance support	Home maintenance support can be claimed if the per capita income in the household does not exceed 150 percent of the minimum old-age pension and the acknowledged costs of housing maintenance exceed 20 percent of the monthly income of the household. In addition, persons participating in a debt management procedure also qualify for this support. Local government can also provide local home maintenance support as an independent benefit or as a supplement. The minimum amount of this support is Ft 2,500 (€9.26) per month.
Poland	Special needs allowance	A person or a family can receive a special needs allowance for housing or heating costs. The amount depends on the decision of social assistance centers.
Romania	Heating benefit	The heating benefit is a seasonal cash transfer program targeted through a means test to households from the poorest half of the population. The program operates mainly for the winter season (November to March). It covers a share of the heating costs, with higher subsidies for households in the lower income brackets. There are three service delivery channels, depending on the type of fuel used for heating: households connected to the central heating grid; households heated with natural gas; and households heating with wood, coal, or crude oil fuels. The amount of the subsidy varies between lei 19 and lei 262.
Russian Federation	Housing and utilities subsidies	Accommodation costs and services are subsidized in accordance with income levels and for certain categories of the population (for example, pensioners, war veterans, invalids). Subsidies are paid in case the cost of accommodation exceeds 20 percent of the income level of the household.

Country	Benefit	Description/eligibility
Serbia	Utilities assistance	Beneficiaries of the material support for families program, depending on the number of family members, are entitled to reduced electricity, water, and other utility bills (reduction ranging between 10 and 40 percent). This reduction falls within the responsibility of the city and municipality governments.
Tajikistan	Electricity and gas compensation	The government compensates households with per capita incomes of less than SM 35 per month per person for electricity and gas. At present, the benefit is 9 dirams (SM 0.09) per KwH. The amount of the benefit is computed equivalent to the cost of a basic allocation for the consumption of KwH of electricity and cubic meters of natural gas. Households that are not attached to the electricity and natural gas grid do not receive these benefits.
Ukraine	Housing subsidies	Reimbursement for cost of household heating is provided for low-income families and based on means testing. A family should not have to pay more than 20 percent of the family income on heating bills. If there are no persons in the family who are capable of work the family should not spend more than 15 percent.

Sources: MISSOC; MISSCEO; World Bank data.

Assessing the Performance of Energy-Related Social Assistance Programs

Social assistance programs are often complex and vary significantly across Eastern Europe and Central Asian countries. These differences are reflected in the design of ESAs. Major differences may include the following:

Eligibility criteria: ESAs can be means tested or categorical.[1] The former focus on the poor or those considered in need. The latter are aimed at groups considered vulnerable or deserving of public support irrespective of their status of economic need. For example, in Ukraine, military personnel, war veterans, Chernobyl victims, and other groups are eligible for discounts on utility bills of up to 100 percent (World Bank 2000; Lovei et al. 2000).

Administration of the benefit. Means-tested energy programs are typically administered by the social assistance system as opposed to the utility or distribution company. In countries with well-developed targeted programs (for example, LRSA and targeted family benefits) with easy certification of beneficiaries, or at least comprehensive registries of beneficiaries, utilities might be able to apply tariff-based measures for customers identified as in need by the social assistance system. Such is the case, for example, of the recently introduced 30 percent discount on the energy bill for recipients of LRSA in Poland.

Degree of integration with other targeted programs. Mean-tested programs can be either a supplement to a targeted program, so that mostly beneficiaries of that program are eligible, or independent programs, potentially with their own means test and other eligibility criteria.[2] Examples of the former include Albania, Estonia, Serbia, and the Slovak Republic. Stand-alone means tested programs are more common (Hungary, Latvia, Lithuania, Poland, and so on). Sometimes these programs use the same means test and certification process and target beneficiaries at higher thresholds (Bulgaria, Adjudor Popular in Moldova). Romania has a hybrid arrangement whereby households heating with wood (in rural areas) receive a supplement of the LRSA, while urban households benefit from a specific energy program.

Type of benefit. Benefits are provided either as cash transfers (for example, Bulgaria and the Slovak Republic) or in kind (for example, Ukraine privileges). Benefits in kind usually represent discounts on utility payments that are paid directly to the utilities on behalf of households, though, sometimes, they are in the form of actual fuel such as coal or wood supplied to beneficiaries or, in more exceptional cases, energy-saving devices such as light bulbs in Tajikistan.[3] Some programs provide a combination of both cash and in-kind benefits. In Latvia, for example, housing benefits are provided as either cash for housing or often in cash or in kind subsidies for winter fuel and, in some cases, in actual housing.

Nature of the benefit. Cash transfer programs can be earmarked to pay the utilities (that is, households are compensated for the bills paid or are provided with vouchers to be redeemed against the payment of bills) or nonearmarked. As for all other benefits, fully fungible benefits are considered theoretically superior to earmarked ones, as they do not risk distorting household consumption patterns. In the case of ESAs, though, especially if the enforcement of payment is weak, earmarked transfers are preferred as they do not create disincentives to pay bills. At the same time, fully fungible transfers could provide incentives to save energy. As pressures for managing demand rise and energy reform progresses so that bill collection is increasingly the responsibility of private operators, such transfers can be expected to become more widespread.

Determination of the benefits. The amount of a benefit is typically either flat (that is, irrespective of actual usage) or proportional to consumption. An example of the former is Romania, where a flat benefit amount (irrespective of actual usage) depends on the per capita income brackets of eligible households and on the type of heating fuel used (central heating, natural gas, wood, coal, or diesel). Similarly, in the Slovak Republic, LRSA beneficiaries receive €55.80 per month for individuals and €89.20 per month for families provided they own or rent accommodations and have proof they have of paid utility bills.[4] A simpler application of this design is the energy benefit recently introduced in FYR Macedonia whereby a flat monthly benefit of €10 is distributed to all beneficiaries of social assistance. An example of a benefit proportional to consumption is the Serbian program, where LRSA recipients are eligible for a discount of 35 percent for the active energy element of the price for up to 450 kWh per month, while customers deemed in a state of extreme social need are eligible to receive a discount of 35 percent for the active energy element of the price for up to 350 kWh per month. A third type of program focuses on limiting the weight of energy expenditures for the household. These programs compensate for the share of utility expenditures that exceeds a notional burden limit, which is set as a given percentage of monthly household income based on actual utility expenditures or on utility expenditure norms. For instance, low-income households in Lithuania should not spend more than 20 percent of the difference between their income and the guaranteed minimum income amount (state-supported income) to heat a standard sized accommodation.

Administration of the program. There are at least two dimensions of the administration of these programs that affect their monetary costs and complexity. First, some programs are designed centrally (at the national level) (Bulgaria, Romania, the Slovak Republic, and so on), while others are designed at the local level (for example, until recently, housing assistance in Latvia varied from municipality to municipality, depending on the available resources.)[5] Second, programs are sometimes funded from national budgets (such as in Bulgaria) and sometimes out of local budgets (Lithuania, Kazakhstan), and sometimes they are cofinanced (Latvia since 2009).

Based on evidence on the subset of countries for which it is possible to analyze performance using the ECAPOV database (see the methodological appendix), the characteristic that appears to matter the most for performance is whether the program is means tested or categorical. Note, however, that, in addition, other important aspects of program design ought to be investigated, including the extent to which these programs provide incentives for wasteful energy consumption or for underreporting income. Such incentives are minimized if transfers are linked to people rather than consumption.[6]

Coverage is low and varies significantly by country:[7] Across the programs examined, coverage ranges from less than 1 percent in Kazakhstan to over 30 percent of the poorest households in Moldova (figure 5.9). In EU MSs, which typically have at least one means-tested social assistance program earmarked for support for housing and energy, coverage ranges from 5 to 15 percent. In EPOC countries, there is considerable variation among the countries that have such programs. Kazakhstan and two of the three programs that exist in Ukraine have low coverage, while the third program, in Ukraine (privileges), and Moldova's nominative compensations have high coverage of the poor, reaching 24 and 31 percent of the population, respectively.

Targeting of the poor is generally greater in the EU countries, where programs are well targeted and progressive.[8] Households in the poorest quintile receive 30–60 percent of the benefits provided. Leakage is low in most countries, with the richest households receiving less than 10 per-

FIGURE 5.9
Housing Program Coverage of Poor Households (Lowest Quintile)

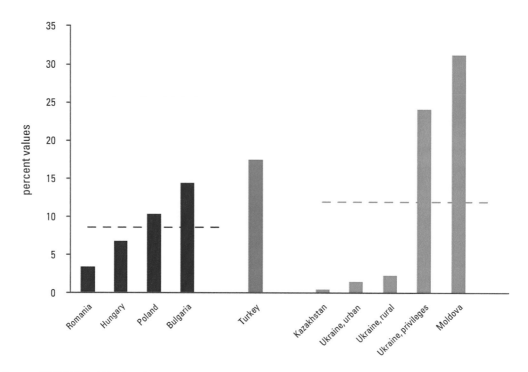

Sources: ECAPOV, World Bank estimates.

cent in most cases. The targeting of Bulgaria's heating allowance stands out, with more than 60 percent of all transfers going to the poorest quintile (figure 5.10).[9] In contrast, in the EPOC countries, programs are much less well targeted on the poor. A stark example is the privileges program in Ukraine, which appears to be strongly regressive. This is worrisome as the program absorbed approximately 0.45 percent of GDP in 2009, equivalent to almost one-fifth of all social assistance spending.[10] Housing and utility allowances in Ukraine are also poorly targeted, as they compensate households for utility expenditures above 20 percent of income. Few of the poor qualify as they spend mostly on food and are less likely to be connected to utilities. Similarly, the program in Kazakhstan is not progressive, as the richest households receive the same share of the benefit as poor households.[11]

Generosity appears to be rather uniform across programs:[12] Housing benefits typically contribute from 5 to 10 percent of total expenditures for the beneficiaries in the poorest households (figure 5.11); Turkey provides a more generous allowance. There is much more variation in generosity across programs if the transfer is expressed as a share of household energy expenditure (from about 30 percent in the case of Hungary to about 100 percent in Ukraine and 96 percent in Russia).

FIGURE 5.10
Distribution of Social Assistance Benefits in Selected Countries

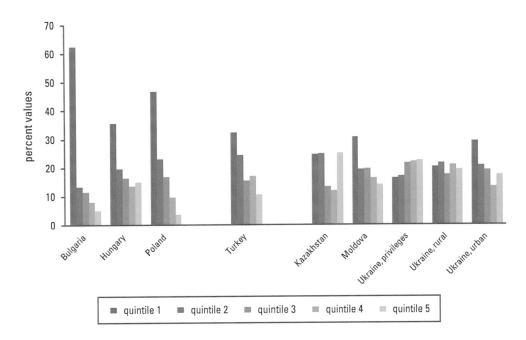

Sources: ECAPOV, World Bank estimates.

FIGURE 5.11
Housing Program Generosity for Poor Households (Lowest Quintile)

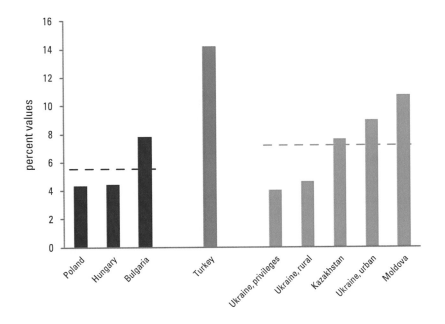

Sources: ECAPOV, World Bank estimates.

Endnotes

1. Means testing can be done either directly (ascertaining the income levels of the potential beneficiaries) or through a proxy means test whereby indicators closely related to income levels, but more easily verified are considered (for example, Armenia, Georgia).
2. Note that, in practice, the distinction between the two, which is useful in describing the overall nature of the system, is blurred. Programs mostly targeted to LRSA beneficiaries often include other groups, such as those vulnerable customers who cannot be disconnected (for example, because of individuals on life-support machines), as in the case of Serbia.
3. Until the winter season 2008/09, this was a feature of heating allowances in Bulgaria. It was reformed to provide only cash support for the heating season irrespective of the type of heating beneficiary due to the high administrative cost of the program, which was previously delivered in kind, and due to recipient feedback about delays in the supply of heating materials, the poor quality of the heating materials, and the undesirable existence of a secondary market for heating vouchers (see World Bank 2009). In Tajikistan, of US$8.3 million budgeted for an electricity and gas compensation program in 2009, at least half was used to purchase and distribute energy-saving lightbulbs (World Bank 2010b).
4. MISSOC (Mutual Information System on Social Protection), January 2010.
5. This benefit did not become a part of mandatory targeted municipal social assistance until 2008.
6. The issue is most acute for programs that subsidize expenditure over a certain threshold, with the threshold expressed as a share of household budget, since the price of an additional unit of electricity, gas, heat, or hot water is effectively zero for a household that reaches the burden limit. Placing a cap on per capita or total household consumption of utility services that counts toward the burden limit, or (even better) using consumption norms to fix the level of utility expenditures for the purpose of benefit calculation can significantly reduce the distortionary effects of such programs.
7. Where coverage is defined as the percentage of households in which at least one member receives benefits from the program.
8. The share of social assistance transfers going to each quintile.
9. This program uses the same means test and certification process as the LRSA program, but target beneficiaries at higher thresholds.
10. ECA Social Protection Database.
11. The errors of inclusion in the program may be explained by the fact that local authorities define the size of and procedure for obtaining housing assistance, as well as the eligibility for the assistance. In this case, richer municipalities or cities can provide substantially higher benefits to relatively more well off households than poor municipalities can.
12. Defined here as the percentage of total (post-transfer) household expenditure constituted by the transfer through the social assistance program.

CHAPTER 6

Balancing Act: Aligning Fiscal and Social Responsibility

This report shows that past investment in infrastructure affects current energy demand patterns and that households would be under significant strain to cope if tariffs were to rise to cost recovery levels. This is a concern at a time when pressures to cut down on subsidies are rising due to fiscal pressures and expectations of additional increases in energy costs. We also argue that rebalancing policy emphasis from subsidies to investments in energy efficiency and more effective social assistance could help households cope and adapt to a higher tariff environment. Business as usual would not be effective in dealing with price shocks of the size we are expecting in most countries in the region. However, while mitigating the impact of higher tariffs and helping households adapt are not going to be cheap, these costs remain below the current levels of subsidies in many countries.

To explore the feasibility of this agenda, this chapter presents policy scenarios that, in their simplicity, help clarify the parameters of the policy choices many countries in Eastern Europe and Central Asia are facing. Our simulations focus on the costs of compensating different groups and of basic energy efficiency programs and show that significant resources would need to be invested. Our simple calculations suggest, however, that an integrated strategy aimed, on the one hand, at ensuring energy affordability to the groups most in need and, on the other hand, at facilitating the transition and adaptation of all households to a new, high energy tariff environment is feasible. Based on rough estimates of the extent to which domestic consumption is currently subsidized, we find that, even putting in place such a comprehensive strategy, could lead to savings of the order of 0.5 to 1 percent of GDP yearly.

The Costs of Compensation

To derive the orders of magnitude of programs aimed at compensating targeted groups of households for energy price increases, we simulate the costs of reaching different groups: the poor, poor households that are energy poor (along the lines of programs used, for example, in Hungary), energy poor households in quintiles 1 and 2, and vulnerable households in quintiles 1 and 2, for both the absolute and the relative definition. Results on the costs of compensating the poor, expressed as a percentage of GDP, are presented in the text, while, for other groups, they are presented in the annex. For the countries on which data are available, we also compare our estimated costs with the cost of existing programs, as well as against our estimate of the benefits in terms of cost savings, that is, the fact that subsidies would no longer be provided.

Our baseline in these simulations is the cost of compensating all households. With estimates ranging from 0 to 4.2 percent of GDP, this baseline might seem too high. While high, our baseline is realistic as these estimates are equivalent to the current budgetary outlay on blanket subsidies for all consumers. Note that, while our estimates on these costs are rudimentary, they are consistent as an order of magnitude with other available estimates of the hidden costs of support to the energy sector.[1]

According to our findings, the cost of compensating poor households is generally low in EU countries due to the low poverty incidence in these countries, whereas the cost is significantly higher in EPOC countries, where the cost of compensation would represent more than 1 percent of GDP in some cases. This is compared to government spending, which, in the region, is often 35–45 percent GDP (see figure 6.1). In most EU countries, the cost of compensating the poor would represent less than 0.2 percent of GDP in most cases. The costliest program would be the one in Bulgaria, where 22 percent of the population is living in poverty (compared with the EU average of 18 percent) and where electricity prices would double (electricity represents more than 60 percent of total energy consumption).

In EPOC countries, where poverty levels average over 50 percent, the cost of compensating the poor would be 50 times more expensive than in EU countries, with an average cost of 0.9 percent of GDP. In the poorest EPOC countries, the cost could be more than 1 percent of GDP. The most extreme example is Armenia, which is almost entirely dependent on electricity and gas (representing more than 95 percent of energy consumption; see annex figure 6.8), is one of the poorest countries in the region (83 percent of the population is living in poverty), and provides some of the highest subsidies. Therefore, if gas and electricity prices more

FIGURE 6.1
Cost of Compensating Poor Households

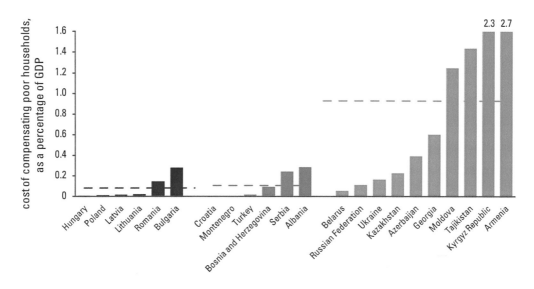

Sources: ECAPOV, World Bank estimates.

than doubled, the cost of compensation for poor households would represent almost 3 percent of GDP. Despite the relatively high levels of poverty in Azerbaijan and Kazakhstan (39 and 48 percent, respectively) and the high price increases, the cost of compensating the poor is relatively low because the shares of energy from electricity and gas are relatively low in these countries (see figure 6.8).

While representing a significant expenditure in some countries, a compensation program targeting the poor would only cover a fraction of the population. Alternative target groups might be considered, especially if they represent constituencies that would be politically vocal and opposed to the reforms. For example, in Bulgaria, which would experience the largest price increase of the EU countries we analyze, a significant number of households in the bottom two quintiles would be pushed into energy poverty or experience a significant jump in their energy bills (that is, they are vulnerable from an absolute perspective). A similar situation is found in Serbia among the CPCs. Figures 6.6–6.8 in the annex illustrate the cost of compensating each of the groups identified above, which would be significantly higher than the cost of targeting only the poor. The costs of compensating other groups amount to an estimated 0.1 to 0.6 percent of GDP for relatively vulnerable quintiles 1 and 2, 0.1 to 0.9 percent of GDP for absolutely vulnerable quintiles 1 and 2, and 0.1 to 2.3 percent of GDP to compensate all households that are both poor and energy poor.

In EPOC countries, in contrast, the poor would be the most expensive group to compensate across those we analyze, especially in countries with the highest levels of poverty. Only in Belarus, Russia and Ukraine would it cost more to compensate vulnerable groups rather than the poor. To get a better sense of the political feasibility of these measures, we compare the cost of compensating poor households against the cost of existing ESAs (where data exist). This provides a helpful indicative benchmark for political feasibility as it reflects what countries are choosing to do right now, irrespective of whether their budgets could support programs of different sizes. (For example, Kazakhstan spends relatively little on ESAs considering the income levels in the country.)

In countries with relatively low levels of poverty (Bosnia and Herzegovina, Croatia, Latvia Montenegro, and Ukraine), the cost of compensating the poor would be lower than the costs of existing ESAs (figure 6.2).[2] In most countries we consider, the cost of compensating all the poor would be out of reach for governments: the cost of compensation would represent more than double the expenditure on existing programs.

FIGURE 6.2
Cost of Compensating Poor Households Versus Existing Energy-Related Programs

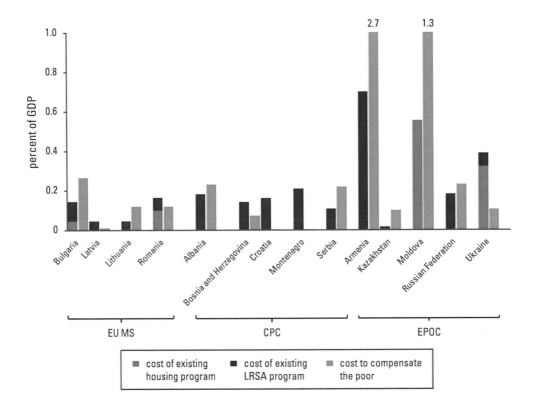

Sources: ECAPOV, World Bank estimates.

In the Balkans, Albania and Serbia would require a compensation program aimed at the poor of the same magnitude of the last resort program, while, in Bosnia and Herzegovina, FYR Macedonia, and Montenegro, the magnitude would remain limited.

Poverty rates are generally higher in EPOC countries, and, in most cases (except Ukraine, a country with limited poverty and a large housing allowance program), compensating all poor households would require a significant increase in existing programs. The extreme example is Armenia, where the compensating program would need to cost around 2.7 percent of GDP, compared with the existing LRSA program, which costs 0.7 percent of GDP.

Investing in Efficiency

As we discuss in chapter 4, demand management is an essential pillar of a policy package to help households adapt and cope with higher energy prices, particularly middle-class households that would not be able to receive direct compensation through ESAs. As we show in chapter 3, a move to cost recovery could lead a significant number of households to experience a large increase in spending on energy. For example, households in the upper three quintiles in the region would experience, on average, a 20 percent increase in the share of spending on energy. In some countries, such as Armenia and Belarus, this increase would be as high as 50 percent.

Given that current consumption patterns are shaped by past investment in infrastructure and housing, it is not surprising that similarly big, long-term investments are needed to shape a new consumption path. To start giving a sense of the payoffs of this type of intervention, we consider a policy scenario whereby the simplest sources of energy inefficiency are addressed (for example, basic insulation, caulking of windows, and so on), something that should be possible with a relatively small outlay per household and that could still lead to as much as a 10 percent reduction in energy demand.

To explore the impacts of such measures, we run a second set of simulations in which we estimate the impact on energy poverty of a demand management policy in the form of a flat US$50 subsidy to a defined beneficiary group. These simulations are not strictly comparable with the previous ones as energy efficiency programs such as this will have a recurring impact. While their benefits are going to be enjoyed for a number of years after the impact, it is also true that, once the easy gains have been made, more consistent investments would be needed to achieve a similar reduction in energy consumption.

As shown in figure 6.3, in EU countries, average household energy shares would be reduced by around 2 percentage points if the program were given to all households. The largest reductions are achieved within the lower quintile households, given that they typically allocate a higher share of spending on energy to begin with (see chapter 2). Similar reductions would be achieved in other parts of the region (see annex 6.1).

The reductions in shares of spending on energy illustrated in figure 6.4 also translate into significant reductions in energy poverty. A 10 percent gain in efficiency would have a much more significant impact in the EPOC countries. In these cases, it may be even more important to undertake an energy efficiency program, together with a compensation program.

FIGURE 6.3

The Impact of Basic Energy Efficiency Programs on Average Energy Shares, by Targeted Quintile, EU MSs

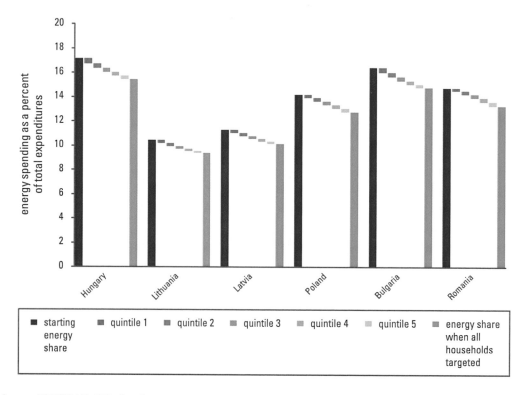

Sources: ECAPOV, World Bank estimates.
Note: The reference for these simulations is based on energy expenditures post increase, before an energy efficiency program is implemented.

FIGURE 6.4
Percent Reduction in Energy Poverty for Poor Households Following the Introduction of an Energy Efficiency Program

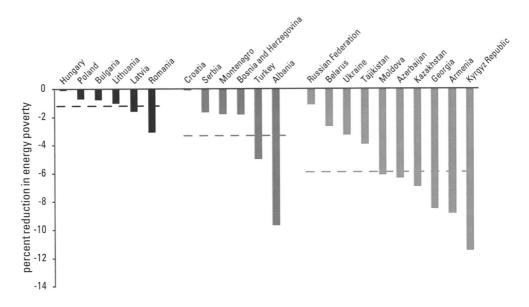

Sources: ECAPOV, World Bank estimates.

The Fiscal Benefits of an Integrated Strategy

As our simple policy scenarios show, the cost of compensating even narrowly defined groups of households for the increase in energy tariffs would be significant in many countries, both as a percentage of GDP and relative to the cost of existing programs. In some cases, these costs may make such compensation and efficiency programs seem prohibitively expensive. But how would the cost of these programs compare to the gains that result from removing implicit subsidies?

In figure 6.5, we estimate the net fiscal net gain each government could expect from pursuing complementary policies to move toward cost recovery by removing subsidies, while also compensating poor households and implementing an efficiency program.[3]

While indicative only, our analysis suggests that significant gains would be generated across the region through the removal of subsidies and protection for poor households. This would leave countries room to identify whether broader protection is needed, particularly during an initial phase when the gains from energy efficiency might still need to materialize. Even in EPOC countries, where implicit subsidies are currently the

FIGURE 6.5

Estimated Net Gains from Removing Subsidies, While Compensating Poor Households and Implementing a Basic Energy Efficiency Program

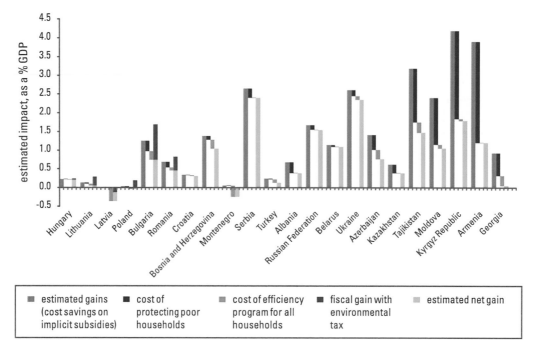

Sources: ECAPOV, World Bank estimates.
Note: estimates are presented as a share of GDP.

highest and where compensation for the poor would be significant, governments in most countries could expect to have a net gain of over 1 percent of GDP[4]. Only two countries—Latvia and Montenegro—would experience a net fiscal loss from this integrated strategy. The opportunity to target energy efficiency interventions more narrowly or to recognize explicitly the investment value of these expenditures would need to be analyzed.

An integrated approach is essential in addressing the political economy challenges of policy change in the energy sector. Global experience tells us that subsidies are often politically difficult to remove once they are in place (box 6.1). Taking an integrated approach whereby the most vulnerable are compensated and all households are helped in managing their energy demand could be an important component in building the political will needed to implement such a change. The net gains of such an approach should form a central part of the communications message for reform, both internal and external to the government.

BOX 6.1
Global Lessons on the Political Economy of Policy Change in the Energy Sector

The political economy of policy change, is critical for policy makers. The removal of energy subsidies will be no exception. Where they exist, energy subsidies tend to be persistent and difficult to remove, and this for a variety of reasons. Most of the literature on the political economy of energy policy reform cites the importance of three elements:

- A government with the political will to implement such change (which usually means a senior figure must champion the reform)
- A strong communications campaign to implement the reform (including communication that subsidies are poorly targeted and mostly go to rich households)
- A multisectoral approach to policy reform, highlighting the complexity of energy subsidies and connecting with multiple ministries. Any policy reform would need to involve internal coordination with all relevant ministries, including the ministry of finance, the ministry of social protection, the ministry of energy, and the ministry of planning

Beyond this high-level guidance, policy makers may need to consider specific and deeper analysis to understand the political economy challenges in their countries and how these challenges may be overcome. This analysis may include the following:

- What are the information gaps among citizens? Often citizens do not know subsidies exist, and, even if they do know, they do not know the generosity of the subsidies. If such information gaps exist, it will be crucial during any transition to communicate current inefficiencies and the nature and benefits of the proposed reform. This can occur even within government ministries. Thus, recently in Romania, the Ministry of Labor increased the coverage of the district heating benefit as they had not realized how much money the government was putting into energy subsidies; perhaps the same information could be made available to citizens. The starting point might be focus groups with a range of citizens to discuss existing information gaps.
- Does the government have credibility? If the removal of subsidies is to be complemented by targeted social assistance or improved electricity service, citizens will need to believe the government will actually follow through. If there is a lack of credibility, the government may need to make the social protection and infrastructure investments up front, before removing subsidies, to avoid any sort of major resistance.
- Are lobbying groups protecting subsidies? Often, a significant portion, if not a majority, of energy subsidies are received by industry and the private sector. Typically, these organizations are well placed to lobby the government to maintain the policy of subsidies. In such cases, it will be important to identify such pressure points and understand if they can be mitigated.

Source: Commander 2011.

Conclusions

The analysis in this report documents the strains that households will face due to higher energy tariffs, particularly if the expected pressures on prices materialize, and the need to shift to a more comprehensive strategy that integrates more effective social assistance interventions with new and more systematic demand management interventions. This final chapter presents several simple policy scenarios to explore the feasibility of such comprehensive policy measures.

Providing compensation to selected groups, even only the poor, would require considerable increases in resources with respect to current budgets. This is in line with the assessment of the previous chapter that existing programs are too small and that the ongoing reforms undertaken in many countries to increase the effectiveness of ESAs offer an opportunity to improve effectiveness and coverage.

Despite their costs, such compensatory measures would leave unattended large parts of the distribution that are likely to be significantly affected by the tariff increases. Demand management measures can help households adapt to higher tariff environments by lowering household demand for energy. These measures can have high payoffs, but typically require significant investments over several years. For the purposes of our simulation, we consider only small one-off interventions that would help households take advantage of opportunities to lower their demand. Subsidizing this type of measure even for the entire distribution would be feasible in most countries in the region. As the savings from cutting budgets would materialize every year, the fiscal space created could help generate more future investment in energy efficiency.

Countries would need to define a path to increasing tariffs and the policy responses necessary to cushion the impacts of such increases in a way that also reflects the readiness and effectiveness of social assistance systems and the time lags involved in making households more resilient to energy price increases through increased efficiency. Overall, however, our simulations show that the energy reforms, accompanied by a coherent response in terms of helping households cope and adapt to tariff increases, could reduce government deficits significantly, by over 1 percent of GDP in almost half of the countries in the region.

Endnotes

1. Our estimates differ from those of Ebinger (2006) and World Bank (2011) because we focus on subsidies to the residential sector only (rather than on the whole), and we do not include other sources of hidden costs such as noncollection and abnormal losses.

2. Note that Ukraine also has a large existing program.
3. Note also that the benefits of efficiency programs will continue beyond the year of investment.
4. In the EPOC countries notable exceptions are Georgia (0.1 percent of GDP), Kazakhstan (0.4 percent of GDP) and Armenia (0.8 percent of GDP).

FIGURE 6.6
Cost of Compensation for Select Target Groups, EU MSs

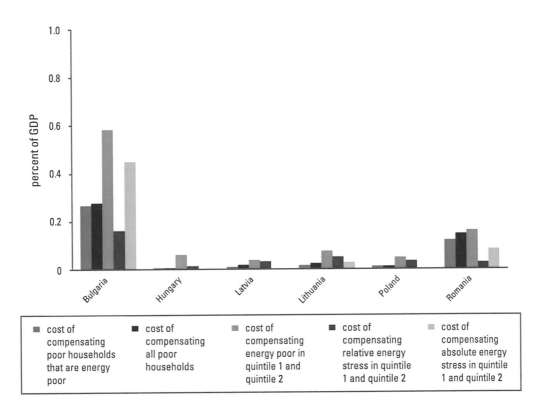

Sources: ECAPOV, World Bank estimates.

FIGURE 6.7
Cost of Compensation for Select Target Groups, CPCs

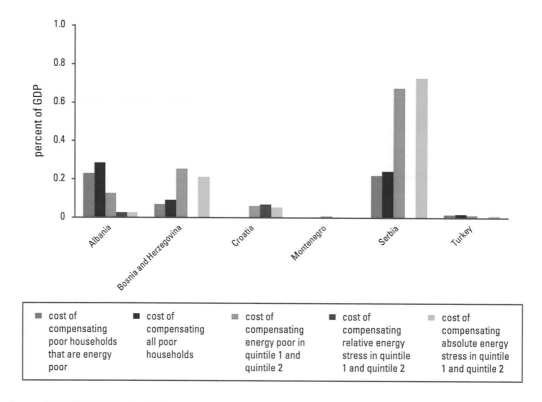

Sources: ECAPOV, World Bank estimates.

FIGURE 6.8

Cost of Compensation for Select Target Groups, EPOC

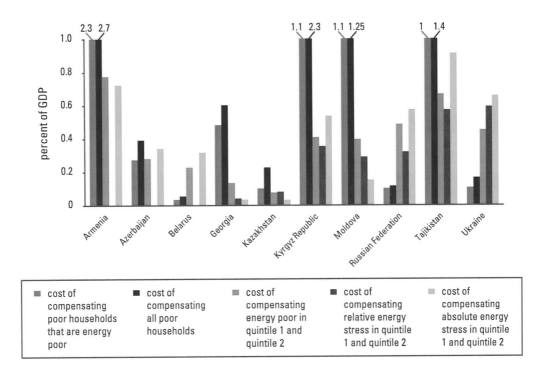

Sources: ECAPOV, World Bank estimates.

Key Definitions

Measures of household welfare

Welfare aggregate: The standardized welfare aggregate used for comparison across Eastern Europe and Central Asia in the ECAPOV database is defined as total expenditure per capita and per year, excluding rent, durables, and health. The aggregate is regionally and quarterly deflated at the country level.

Income and income groups, quintiles: Given the unequal coverage of income variables across the household surveys in the region, we use the ECAPOV welfare aggregate discussed above as a proxy for income and to identify relevant subgroups (income groups, quintiles).

Poor: A household is considered poor if its total expenditures, excluding rent, durables, and health, are below purchasing power parity US$5 per capita and per day.

Energy poor: A household is considered energy poor if its total energy expenditure is equal or greater than 10 percent of its total expenditure.

Energy stress (absolute): A household is deemed in energy stress due to an energy price increase if its energy expenditure increase, following the electricity or gas price increase to cost recovery, is above the cost of 100 kWh/month at the pre-increase price.

Energy stress (relative): A household is deemed relatively vulnerable to an energy price increase if its energy share increase, following the electricity or gas price increase to cost recovery, is above 1.5 times the median increase in the share.

Measures of energy tariffs and consumption

Average price for residential users: We adopt the ERRA database estimates of average prices for residential users for electricity and gas, where available; these rely on dividing total residential bills by total consumption. This is an approximation of tariffs, which are often designed as block tariffs. The approximation is most accurate if prices are linear or quasi-linear. If the fixed part of the tariff is significant, the actual average price per unit will be underestimated for low-consumption users and overestimated for high-consumption users. In the case of an increasing block tariff, the average price will be overestimated for low-consumption users and underestimated for high-consumption users. For Tajikistan which was not covered by the ERRA database, we used a tariff from the EBRD Transition Report (EBRD 2010).

Cost recovery: We adopt a regional standard for cost recovery of 12.5 U.S. cents/kWh for electricity (16 U.S. cents/kWh if environmental costs are taken into account, which we assume to be the case in EU-10 countries) and US$560/1,000 m^3 (that is, US$16.70/GJ) for gas. This standard is based on estimates of the price of generation at gas-fired plants, which are typically the marginal plants used to face peak demand. These targeted cost recovery prices are excluding tax.

Price increase to cost recovery level: The simulated price increase to electricity and gas cost recovery levels is based on the distance between country average residential price and the average cost recovery price. However, for the plausibility of the simulations, the increase has been capped to 200 percent when the estimated increase is beyond this figure. We have not simulated a simultaneous increase in the price of central heating because of a lack of common reference for the region. The impact of this omission for countries where central heating represents a significant share of energy expenditures (especially among wealthiest households) are discussed in methodological appendix B.

Electricity and gas consumption: Electricity and gas consumption is estimated based on the total annual expenditure for each energy source and the average price for residential users, including taxes. The limitations of relying on average prices applies here as well: underestimated unit prices will lead to an overestimate of consumption, and vice versa. In addition, our estimates are affected by problems with reported energy expenditures, such as nonpayment, or possible fines or other expenditures not linked to actual consumption that households might have to pay. In the case of gas, network gas and liquefied petroleum gas (LPG) are expenditures are not always differentiated. In Azerbaijan in particular, network gas and LPG expenditures are recorded together. The gas consumption has been estimated for households with positive gas expenditures, under the assumption that all gas expenditures are network gas, but this might overestimate the actual network gas consumption.

Measures of performance of social assistance programs

Energy-related social assistance programs (ESA, or energy programs): In the empirical analysis, which relies on household reported social assistance, we include programs that typically included "housing" or "heating" in the program name. Note that only some of the earmarked transfer programs for housing or heating are captured through the household surveys included in the ECAPOV database. Note that some programs were too small to be included in the analysis (for example, Latvia and Lithuania); other programs are difficult to identify. Energy programs delivered through existing LRSA programs have not been included as it is difficult isolate them in the data.

Quintiles of the pretransfer welfare distribution: For the purpose of identifying the performance of existing social programs, quintiles are derived from the pretransfer distribution (measured as total expenditures, minus the amount of the transfers). These quintiles are different from those applied in the rest of the analysis, where they are derived from the post-transfer distribution (that is, from total expenditures as measured by the ECAPOV welfare aggregate), but are more appropriate to the analysis of social assistance programs.

Coverage: Percentage of households where at least one member receives benefits from the program.

Targeting: The share of social assistance transfers going to each quintile.

Generosity: Unless otherwise specified, generosity is defined as the percentage of total (post-transfer) household expenditure constituted by the transfer through the social assistance program.

Methodology

The main analytical tool applied in this study is the comparison of actual and simulated energy expenditures shares after the tariff increase across the welfare distribution and the corresponding energy poverty distribution.

The descriptive analysis in chapter 3 compares actual consumption patterns as reported in the household surveys (Living Standards Measurement Studies [LSMS] and Household Budget Survey [HBS]) collected between 2007 and 2010. Per capita household expenditures as standardized in the ECAPOV database are used for the distributional analysis of consumption. This standardized variable includes all expenditures except durables, health expenditures, and rent. Households are ranked and divided into five groups of equal size (quintiles) in each country, based on total household expenditures per capita, unless indicated otherwise. As discussed in greater detail in methodological appendix D, standardizing the energy expenditure aggregates required addressing problems related to hot water and wood consumption, as well as seasonality.

The simulations on the price increases presented in chapter 4 consider the impacts of a rise in electricity and gas tariffs to cost recovery levels in terms of increases in the share of energy expenditures, poverty status, and energy poverty status. Taking into account that households may adjust their consumption behavior by reducing their energy use or switching to other fuels, we correct post-increase electricity and gas consumption by assuming an average price elasticity of −0.25. All other expenditures are kept at the initial level.

To estimate the impact of the change in tariffs on the share of energy expenditures in total household expenditures, we calculate the change in the electricity share and in the gas share. This change can be calculated as follows:

$$\Delta S\_el = S\_el_1 \, . \, S\_el_0 = (S\_el_0(P_1-P_0)/P_0)(\varepsilon + \varepsilon(P_1-P_0)/P_0 + 1) - S\_el_0$$

$$\Delta S\_el = (S\_el_0 * \Delta P/P)(\varepsilon + \varepsilon(\Delta P/P + 1) - S\_el_0 \quad (B.1)$$

Thus:

$$S\_energy_1 = S\_energy_0 + \Delta S\_el + \Delta S\_gas, \quad (B.2)$$

where S_el_0, S_gas_0, and S_energy_0 are the electricity, gas, and energy shares before the price change; P_0 and P_1 are the tariffs before and after the increase ($\Delta P/P$ is the price increase to cost recovery); and ε is the price elasticity of demand.

Following Freund and Wallich (1995), we calculate the loss in the consumer surplus as a share of the total expenditures associated with the higher energy tariffs, defined as follows:[1]

$$\Delta CS\_el \, / \, E = [Q\_el_0(p_1-p_0)(\, 1 + \varepsilon(p_1-p_0)/2p_0)] \, / \, E,$$

$$\Delta CS\_gas \, / \, E = [Q\_gas_0(p_1-p_0)(\, 1 + \varepsilon(p_1-p_0)/2p_0)] \, / \, E,$$

$$\Delta CS/ \, E = \Delta CS\_el \, / \, E + \Delta CS\_gas \, / \, E, \quad (B.3)$$

where E is total household expenditures and Q_el_0 and Q_gas_0 are the initial quantity of electricity and gas consumed.

The analysis of social assistance programs in chapter 5 is based on the ECAPOV database, using reported social assistance received by households. This is possible because a number of countries have created earmarked transfer programs for housing or heating, with eligibility criteria distinct from the last resort social assistance program (LRSA). A number of these are captured through household surveys. Typically, programs that included "housing" or "heating" in their title were included.

There are some limitations to this analysis because household surveys do not cover all programs. Some programs are too small to be included. Other programs are difficult to identify. If support is provided through existing LRSA programs, it is difficult to isolate and compare the contribution to household welfare. As a result, social assistance programs that are integrated in income support programs are not considered in this analysis. The scope of our analysis focuses on direct benefits (cash or in kind) and does not include universal benefits provided through subsidies. A number of countries were also omitted from the analysis because sample sizes were so small, for example, Latvia and Lithuania.

As a result of the methodology described above and its limitations, a subset of eight countries in the Eastern Europe and Central Asia region, covering 10 programs, were included in the analysis: Bulgaria (heating allowance), Hungary (housing support), Poland (housing benefit), Romania (heating benefit), Turkey (annual direct transfer for gas payment), Moldova (nominative compensations for heating, gas, electricity, and communication services), Kazakhstan (housing allowance), and Ukraine, including (1) housing and utility privileges and (2) housing and utility allowance (rural and urban).

Note that the methodology for grouping households into quintiles varies slightly from other sections of the report because quintiles are identified based on pretransfer consumption, while other parts of the report base quintiles on post-transfer consumption. This slightly different definition, which is more appropriate in the analysis of the performance of social assistance, implicitly assumes that household social assistance program receipts do not affect private transfer receipts or household labor market behavior.

Endnotes

1. Compensating variation and equivalent variation are two different ways to measure the effect of a change in the price of one good relative to other goods. *Compensating variation* is the amount of money that would have to be given to a consumer to offset completely the harm from a price increase. *Equivalent variation* is the amount of money that would have to be taken from a consumer to harm the consumer by as much as the price increase. These concepts are difficult to estimate in practice. The change in consumer surplus, which does not hold a consumer's utility constant, thus reflects both the substitution and income effects and is a good approximation of the other two measures.

Sensitivity of the Results to Changes in the District Heating Tariffs in Countries in Which Central Heating Is a Significant Share of Total Energy Consumption

Because there is no central heating prices database for international comparison, the main thrust of this report has focused on simulating tariff increases only for electricity and gas prices. Detailed studies on district heating are being conducted on a country basis (see, for example, World Bank 2011a).

It is unlikely that countries would implement cuts in subsidies without addressing also subsidies through the district heating system. This appendix therefore explores the sensitivity of the results presented in the main text to simulated district heating increases. The simulations underestimate the effects of energy price increases in countries in which central heating represents a significant share of total energy expenditures. In addition, because central heating is more regularly consumed by wealthier households relative to poorer households, the distributive impact is likely to be biased by the omission of central heating from the simulations.

The order of magnitude simulated is purely theoretical and is used so as to obtain a sense of broad distributional patterns. We assume that the price of central heating increases in the same proportion as gas. Where the gas price is unknown or the gas price is already at or close to cost recovery, an increase of 50 percent is simulated. Table 6.1 summarizes the findings of this sensitivity analysis.

In Bulgaria and Hungary, where central heating represents, respectively, 9 and 11 percent of the average energy expenditures, the energy

TABLE 6.1

Sensitivity Analysis of the Energy Share Increase under Different Assumptions on the Tariff Increase for Central Heating (percent values)

Country (year)	Central heating as share of total energy	Total energy share	Electricity tariff increase	Gas tariff increase	Total energy share increase		
					Without central heating tariff increase	Central heating tariff increase = gas price increase	Central heating tariff: +50%
Bulgaria 2007	9.08	12.76	98.94	44.04	29.56	32.17	32.45
Hungary 2007	10.72	16.41	1.78	18.79	4.92	6.36	8.32
Kazakhstan 2007	17.34	8.031	197.3		16.98		24.87
Latvia 2009	25.97	10.74	21.9	0	7.13	7.13	18.61
Lithuania 2008	23.18	9.392	49.13	4.95	15.28	16.51	25.89
Poland 2009	17.42	13.54	15.13	5.17	5.10	5.97	12.25
Russian Federation 2008	22.1	8.02	136	200	33.59	50.79	44.34
Ukraine 2008	26.1	6.32	200	200	30.29	43.83	38.75

Sources: ECAPOV, World Bank estimates.

share increase would be significantly higher if the central heating price rises in the same proportion as the gas price (table 6.1). As for the distributional impacts, the energy share increase due to the electricity and gas price increase is already higher among wealthier households, and this pattern would be reinforced by the central heating price increase (table 6.2).

In Kazakhstan, the Russian Federation, and Ukraine, where central heating represents more than 17 percent of total energy expenditures, the distributive pattern of the impact of electricity and gas price increases is the opposite relative to Bulgaria and Hungary because the poorest households incur the highest energy share increase. However, if the price of central heating also rises in the same proportion as the gas price increase (or 50 percent in the case of Kazakhstan), the energy share increase would be greater for wealthier households relative to poorer households. No data are available for central heating in Belarus.

In Latvia and Poland, where the gas price increase to cost recovery would remain limited, a 50 percentage increase of the price of central heating would also reverse the distributive impact of the price increase and affect the wealthiest households more than the poorest households. In Lithuania, the impact of the increase would be uniform.

TABLE 6.2
Sensitivity Analysis of the Energy Share Increase under Different Assumptions on the Tariff Increase for Central Heating, by Quintile

Quintile	Central heating as a share of total energy	Total energy share	Electricity price increase	Gas price increase	Total energy share increase		
					Without central heating price increase	Central heating price increase = gas price increase	Central heating price: +50%
Bulgaria							
Quintile 1	5.837	15.97	.9894	.4404	.2875	.3043	.3061
Quintile 2	9.796	14.37	.9894	.4404	.2882	.3163	.3194
Quintile 3	9.216	12.58	.9894	.4404	.2928	.3192	.3221
Quintile 4	9.265	11.44	.9894	.4404	.3057	.3323	.3352
Quintile 5	11.27	9.467	.9894	.4404	.304	.3364	.3399
Total	9.077	12.76	.9894	.4404	.2956	.3217	.3245
Hungary							
Quintile 1	4.34	20.88	.01775	.1879	.03829	.04411	.05206
Quintile 2	7.619	17.6	.01775	.1879	.04791	.05813	.07209
Quintile 3	11.06	16.24	.01775	.1879	.05159	.06642	.08667
Quintile 4	13.04	14.77	.01775	.1879	.05374	.07123	.09512
Quintile 5	17.52	12.57	.01775	.1879	.05451	.07801	.1101
Total	10.72	16.41	.01775	.1879	.04921	.06358	.08321
Kazakhstan							
Quintile 1	7.362	9.193	1.973	.	.1917	.	.2247
Quintile 2	12.86	8.52	1.973	.	.1714	.	.2303
Quintile 3	17.69	8.47	1.973	.	.1607	.	.2417
Quintile 4	22.21	7.5	1.973	.	.1628	.	.2635
Quintile 5	26.58	6.47	1.973	.	.1627	.	.2832
Total	17.34	8.031	1.973	.	.1698	.	.2487

Quintile	Central heating as a share of total energy	Total energy share	Electricity price increase	Gas price increase	Total energy share increase		
					Without central heating price increase	Central heating price increase = gas price increase	Central heating price: +50%
Russian Federation							
Quintile 1	14.72	10.89	1.36	2	.3889	.4976	.4568
Quintile 2	21.93	9.374	1.36	2	.3409	.5065	.4444
Quintile 3	24.09	8.086	1.36	2	.318	.5081	.4368
Quintile 4	25.93	6.451	1.36	2	.3114	.5128	.4373
Quintile 5	26.27	3.84	1.36	2	.3021	.5191	.4377
Total	22.1	8.019	1.36	2	.3359	.5079	.4434
Ukraine							
Quintile 1	15.67	7.449	2	2	.3351	.4164	.386
Quintile 2	20.98	6.978	2	2	.3156	.4244	.3836
Quintile 3	24.74	6.297	2	2	.3117	.44	.3919
Quintile 4	31.01	5.85	2	2	.2893	.4502	.3899
Quintile 5	38.05	5.019	2	2	.2627	.4602	.3861
Total	26.1	6.319	2	2	.3029	.4383	.3875
Latvia							
Quintile 1	14.26	11.76	.219	0	.09007	.09007	.1565
Quintile 2	22.49	11.5	.219	0	.07857	.07857	.1773
Quintile 3	28.98	11.95	.219	0	.06687	.06687	.1944
Quintile 4	31.58	10.6	.219	0	.06149	.06149	.1989
Quintile 5	32.49	7.852	.219	0	.05972	.05972	.2033
Total	25.97	10.74	.219	0	.07133	.07133	.1861
Lithuania							
Quintile 1	14	11.37	.4913	.04946	.1882	.1964	.2581
Quintile 2	24.73	11.52	.4913	.04946	.1516	.1643	.2598
Quintile 3	24.54	9.859	.4913	.04946	.1481	.1611	.2597
Quintile 4	25.83	7.917	.4913	.04946	.1442	.1578	.2611
Quintile 5	26.7	6.293	.4913	.04946	.1321	.1466	.2559
Total	23.18	9.392	.4913	.04946	.1528	.1651	.2589
Poland							
Quintile 1	9.72	12.33	.1513	.05173	.0555	.0603	.09484
Quintile 2	14.51	13.43	.1513	.05173	.05442	.06163	.1135
Quintile 3	17.56	14.18	.1513	.05173	.05183	.06059	.1236
Quintile 4	20.35	14.26	.1513	.05173	.04935	.05951	.1326
Quintile 5	24.17	13.52	.1513	.05173	.0445	.05679	.1452
Total	17.42	13.54	.1513	.05173	.05101	.05973	.1225

Sources: ECAPOV, World Bank estimates.

References

World Bank. 2011a. "Modernization of the District Heating Systems in Ukraine: Heat Metering." Unpublished report, World Bank, Washington, DC.

The ECAPOV Database and the Standardization of Energy Variables

The microlevel information at the core of this report is taken from the ECAPOV database of standardized household surveys. The ERRA database of tariffs serves as the main source for tariff data. The ECAPOV household surveys dataset available for the analysis of energy expenditures covers 23 countries, mainly through household budget surveys, with one to four surveys per country for the period 2002–09. The most recent surveys available in the database by country are detailed in table 6.3. For the purpose of this analysis, no survey prior to 2007 has been used, thereby excluding Estonia, for which only 2004 data are available, as well as Kosovo.

TABLE 6.3

The Most Recent Surveys Available in the ECAPOV Database

EU MSs	Western Balkans and Turkey, CPCs	EPOC countries
Bulgaria (2007)	Albania (2008)	Armenia (2009)
Estonia (2004)	Bosnia and Herzegovina (2007)	Azerbaijan (2008)
Hungary (2007)	Kosovo (2006)	Belarus (2009)
Latvia (2009)	Macedonia, FYR (2009)	Kazakhstan (2007)
Lithuania (2008)	Montenegro (2009)	Georgia (2008)
Poland (2009)	Serbia (2009)	Kyrgyz Republic (2008)
Romania (2009)	Turkey (2009)	Moldova (2009)
Croatia (2008)		Russian Federation (2008)
		Tajikistan (2009)
		Ukraine (2008)

The ECA households survey database provides standardized sociode-mographic information at the household and individual levels (house-hold structure, educational attainment, professional activities, and, sometimes, ethnicity), as well as annual expenditure aggregates. Utility expenditures are standardized as part of the ECAPOV welfare aggregate (total utility expenditures are defined as the sum of electricity, gas, total fuels, central heating, water, waste, and other utilities).

The reference welfare aggregate for the ECAPOV database includes all expenditures, apart from health and rent. It is adjusted for yearly infla-tion and for regional differences. Poor households are identified based on the upper ECAPOV poverty line (US$5 a day), expressed in local currency based on the data of the 2005 International Comparison Program data (icp2005) of the World Bank and updated over time using the consumer price index.

Identification and standardization of energy expenditures

In addition to the standardized variables already contained in the ECAPOV database, energy expenditure variables have been further standardized using the construction of an energy expenditures aggregate (adjusted for regional and quarter price differences and normalized as in the case of the total expenditures aggregate) and related share variable (energy expen-ditures as a share of total expenditures), as well as the breakdown of energy expenditures (each type of energy expenditure as a share of total energy expenditures) (see table 6.5).

While most surveys are quite standardized, energy expenditures might vary across surveys in terms of the following:

- Recall periods vary between grid utilities (gas, electricity, and central heating) and fuels.

- Network gas and LPG expenditures are usually distinct, except for Azerbaijan, Belarus, and Bulgaria, where a single expenditure is recorded.

- Central heating is usually district heating, but sometimes includes hot water (Estonia, Serbia, Turkey, and Ukraine), or a heating pipe in the bathroom (Lithuania); thus, energy expenditures cannot be exclu-sively identified for these countries (table 6.5). In Belarus, district heating cannot be identified from the other housing expenditures.

- Wood expenditures represent only purchased goods to be consistent across surveys. However, in some countries where wood self-con-sumption is an important energy source, such as in the Balkans, this expenditure may be included in the total welfare aggregate. This is the case of Montenegro.

Caveats and assumptions

Nonresponse. In some countries, a significant number of households present no expenditures at all for any utility. The most concerning case is FYR Macedonia, where 50 percent of households are recorded with zero utility expenditures. In all other surveys, utility nonresponse is lower, but still noticeable. For example, it reached 13 percent in Azerbaijan in 2008, 7.3 percent in Turkey, and 6.6 percent in Poland. Poorer households are more likely to show nonresponse for utility variables than other groups, with the exception of Hungary, Azerbaijan, and the Kyrgyz Republic (table 6.4). Some of these nonresponses might truly correspond to zero expenditure (for all kind of utilities) due to nonpayment. Indeed, Lampietti et al. (2007), based on complementary utility data, find that no expenditure for a utility is positively correlated with the consumption level as a ratio of total expenditure, especially in Albania, Armenia, Russia, Tajikistan, and Turkey. Nonresponse for nongrid components of the ECAPOV utility aggregate (and, in particular, fuel) are more difficult to explain. In some cases, the survey design appears to play a key role. For example, in FYR Macedonia, the recall period for utilities is only two weeks, while fieldwork takes place continuously during the month. If households tend to pay their bills at the same time (for example, at the beginning of the month, when they receive the bills), households that are interviewed after more than two weeks after the payments cannot provide information on their utility expenditure.[1] For fuels like wood and coal, there might be strong seasonality patterns, as households are likely to buy large quantities once or twice a year, usually just before winter. While grid utilities are usually monthly expenditures, the seasonality pattern of fuel expenditures in particular is addressed heterogeneously across surveys: most surveys only record the last month or the last three months of expenditures (Armenia, Bosnia and Herzegovina, Georgia, Kazakhstan, Lithuania, Moldova, Montenegro, Romania, Russia, Serbia, Turkey, and Ukraine). Where solid fuels represent a high proportion of the heating source (Bosnia and Herzegovina, Moldova, Montenegro, Romania, Serbia, and Turkey), fuel expenditures are likely to be missed for some households and overestimated for the ones that report them. Few surveys record 12 months of expenditures for fuels (Azerbaijan, Bulgaria, Croatia, and the Kyrgyz Republic), and only two surveys distinguish between monthly winter and summer expenditures: Albania and Tajikistan. This specific caveat is detailed for each survey where relevant.

In processing the data, based on the available documentation and, wherever possible, expert advice, we had to make a number of assumptions. These are detailed below.

TABLE 6.4
Distribution of the No Energy Expenditures Pattern across Quintiles (percent values)

Country (year)	No energy expenditure	Distribution of the households with no energy expenditures				
	All	Quintile 1	Quintile 2	Quintile 3	Quintile 4	Quintile 5
EU MS						
Bulgaria 2007	0.11	64.29	21.43	7.14	7.14	0
Estonia 2004	8.59	45.89	12.3	17.36	13.95	10.5
Hungary 2007	0.10	28.25	19.6	13.2	12.6	26.35
Latvia 2009	0.17	56.84	13.01	25.68	4.46	0
Lithuania 2008	1.36	34.27	23.63	10.75	11.76	19.6
Poland 2009	6.58	37.38	21.87	15.97	13.7	11.08
Romania 2009	2.98	60.04	20.37	9.62	6.28	3.69
CPC countries						
Albania 2008	1.79	56.27	22.62	9.63	9.49	1.98
Bosnia and Herzegovina 2007	0.22	84.91	9.29	1.97	1.85	1.97
Macedonia, FYR 2009	49.89	33.5	26.56	20.68	12.32	6.95
Montenegro 2009	1.45	51	6.42	31.18	9.57	1.83
Serbia 2009	2.74	71.58	9.27	5.79	8.79	4.56
Turkey 2009	7.28	58.29	21.56	8.85	5.95	5.36
CIS						
Armenia 2009	0.03	41.22	26.32	32.46	0	0
Azerbaijan 2008	12.79	22.4	16.58	20.13	20.62	20.27
Belarus 2009	2.53	24.69	26.56	19.04	14.63	15.09
Georgia 2008	2.76	43.26	25.31	17.93	7.27	6.22
Kazakhstan 2007	0.49	23.27	5.28	19.92	22.3	29.23
Kyrgyz Republic 2008	1.28	5.33	4.64	22.08	16.7	51.25
Moldova 2009	0.13	76.42	0	6.42	17.16	0
Russian Federation 2008	4.44	30.48	18.12	14.57	16.76	20.07
Tajikistan 2009	0.10	67.35	32.65	0	0	0
Ukraine 2008	0.29	42.33	13.79	13.02	18.03	12.82

Sources: ECAPOV, World Bank estimates.

Azerbaijan 2008. Gas is assumed to be network gas (LPG and gas are recorded jointly), and gas expenditure is used to estimate gas consumption based on residential gas unit price.

Armenia 2009. The main heating source is gas. While 29 percent of the households use wood for heating, only 0.4 percent report wood expenditures. Monthly data show a high seasonality pattern for wood expenditures (wood expenditures are mainly reported in October and November).

Belarus 2009. Energy expenditures are assumed to be annualized household expenditures, repeated in the individual file for every household member (thus, averaged for household estimates). Electricity and fuels are reported separately from the other housing and utility expenditures, which include most probably district heating in addition to water, garbage collection and other municipal services. Total identified energy variables (electricity, gas, wood, coal and peat) are thus far lower than the total housing variable and is likely to be incomplete. Gas is assumed to be network gas, and gas expenditure is used to estimate gas consumption based on the residential gas unit price.

Bosnia and Herzegovina 2007. Wood is the main source for heating (for 85 percent of the households), however only 25 percent report wood expenditures during the last 3 months due to the seasonality pattern of such expenditures (in addition to own production wood).

Bulgaria 2007. Gas is assumed to be network gas, and gas expenditure is used to estimate gas consumption based on the residential gas unit price (gas expenditures are limited in any case).

Georgia 2008. 8,606 households in the energy file are not in the aggregate ECAPOV file. Only the aggregate ECAPOV file is retained for reference. Wood expenditures display a high seasonality pattern (only 8 percent report wood expenditures during the last three months).

Kazakhstan 2007. Wood and coal expenditures are recorded for the last 3 months and display high seasonality patterns.

Kyrgyz Republic 2008. Monthly expenditures have been summed without correction for missing months, as per the poverty file. Data are consistent with the poverty file.

FYR Macedonia 2008. 45 percent of households have no reported expenditures for housing; this share is 80 percent among the poorest quintile. These missing expenditures are observed irrespective of the main heating source (electricity, central heating, or wood). Energy poverty rates are affected. The reduced sample with expenditures is not representative (7 percent in quintiles 1; 33 percent in quintile 5).

Moldova 2009. Solid fuel is the main heating source and a limited proportion of households report wood or coal expenditures for the last month.

Montenegro 2009. The three-months expenditure file and the diary are used; however, 78.3 percent of households still report only electricity expenditures while 70 percent use solid fuel for heating. Wood from own household plots is not included in the total so as to remain consistent with other surveys, while it is probably included in the total expenditures aggregate (21 percent of households report such an equivalent expenditure; if it were included, this would add 1.2 percent to the total energy share).

Poland 2009. Most of the household using solid fuel for heating do not report any expenditures for wood or coal and a high seasonality pattern for such fuel expenditures is assumed. Only 5 percent of the household report wood expenditures. Wood and coal expenditures as a share of total expenditures are high for these rare households once annualized.

Romania 2009. The monthly wood expenditures display a high seasonality pattern. Only 9 percent of the household report wood expenditures during the last month, while 48 percent use solid fuel for heating. Wood expenditures as a share of total expenditures is high for these rare households once annualized.

Russia 2008. Utilities are assumed to be monthly expenditures (water, electricity, gas, central). No assumption is made for fuels, and these are summed quarterly. Quarterly wood and coal expenditures display a high seasonality pattern. Only 3 percent of the household report wood or coal expenditures. Wood and coal expenditures as a share of total expenditures is high for these rare households once annualized based on the quarterly expenditures.

Serbia 2009. Solid fuel is a major heating source, however only 20 percent of the households heating with solid fuels report wood expenditures during the last 3 months (14 percent for coal expenditures).

Tajikistan 2009. 7 percent of households use network gas for heating, but the gas expenditure variable is missing (the questionnaire does not include the question). Energy data display high seasonality patterns between the summer and the winter seasons: the assumption for the total energy expenditures is that each season lasts 6 months (winter and summer monthly expenditures are expanded 6 times).

Turkey 2009. 7 percent of households report no energy expenditure; this share rises to 21 percent in the poorest quintile.

Caution is also required as currency changes are taken into account in within-country comparisons, as well as in the conversion to international dollars in the comparisons across countries, as follows:

- Albania: 1 new lek = 10 old lek since 2008

- Azerbaijan: 1 new azerimanat = 5,000 old manat since 2006

- Romania: 1 RON = 10 000 ROL since 2005

Endnotes

1. Note that, for the purposes of national accounting, the overall energy expenditure of the household sector is calculated by doubling the estimates of the survey. While the shortfalls of the recall periods can be addressed at the aggregate level, it is not possible in microanalysis.

TABLE 6.5
Inventory and Characteristics of the Energy Expenditures in the most Recent Surveys

Survey	Type	Number of households in ECAPOV file	Households with no housing expenditure (%)	Households with no energy expenditure (zero) (%)	Share of housing in total expenditure (%)	Share of utility in total expenditure (%)	Share of energy in total expenditure (%)
Albania 2008	LSMS	3599	1.0	1.8	12.56	11.64	10.53
Armenia 2009	ILCS	7872	0.1	0.0	10.42	10.53	9.47
Azerbaijan 2008	LSMS	5587	13.3	12.8	7.77	7.22	6.70
Belarus 2009	HHS	5027	0.2	2.5	9.57		3.60
Bosnia and Herzegovina 2007	HBS	7468	0.3	0.2	10.12	10.00	8.87
Bulgaria 2007	MTHS	4300	0.2	0.1	15.25	15.26	12.78
Croatia 2008	HBS	3108	0.8	0.9	17.25	11.03	9.29
Estonia 2004	HBS	3165	4.8	8.6	19.03	10.54	10.10
Georgia 2008	HBS	11063	2.8	2.8	12.36	11.54	10.93
Hungary 2007	HBS	8547	0.1	0.1	18.89	20.25	16.41
Kazakhstan 2007	HBS	12000	0.4	0.5	9.34	8.94	7.55
Kyrgyz Republic 2008	HBS	4995	0.7	1.3	9.19	8.00	7.35
Latvia 2009	HBS	4359	0.1	0.2	15.44	12.93	9.56
Lithuania 2008	HBS	6102	1.1	1.4	13.54	10.97	8.38
Moldova 2009	HBS	5532	0.2	0.1	16.23	16.11	14.60
Macedonia, FYR 2009	HBS	4011	45	50	8.37	3.87	3.31

Frequency of info on energy expenditure	Energy expenditures identified	Treatment of gas and LPG	Collected Wood
Monthly (winter/summer except electricity and gas)	Electricity, LPG, wood, coal, oil, kerosene, diesel, other fuel	Gas is assumed to be LPG	No data
Last month	Electricity, gas, LPG, wood, coal, dry spirit, Kerosene, diesel, candles, central	Gas AND LPG	No data
Annual and quarterly	Electricity, gas, wood, coal, liquid central	Gas assumed to be network gas	No data
Annualized	Electricity, gas, wood, coal, peat, other fuel – central heating in housing /municipal services	Gas is LPG or network gas	No data
Last month/ quarterly	Electricity, gas, LPG, liquid, wood, coal, central	Gas AND LPG (limited)	No data
Annual	Electricity, gas, liquid, wood, coal, central	Gas is LPG or network gas	
Mainly monthly/ annual for fuels	Electricity, gas, LPG, wood, coal, liquid, central	Gas AND LPG	
Monthly	Electricity, gas, LPG, wood, coal, briquets, liquid, other fuels, w-central (w-central heating is combined with hot water, steam and ice)	Gas AND LPG	No data
Quarterly	Electricity, gas, LPG, wood, coal, kerosene, diesel, other fuel	Gas AND LPG	No data
Annualized	Electricity, gas, LPG, wood, coal, liquid, central	Gas AND LPG	In questionnaire
Quarterly	Electricity, gas, LPG, wood, coal, solid, peat, kerosene, diesel, heating oil, other fuel, central	Gas AND LPG	In questionnaire
Monthly/annually	Electricity, gas, LPG, wood, coal, peat, kerosene, heating oil, agricultural residue, liquid, central	Gas AND LPG	In questionnaire
Annualized	Electricity, gas, LPG, liquid, central	Gas AND LPG	
Monthly	Electricity, gas, LPG, liquid, wood, coal, peat, w-central (w-central includes "sildymas", "silumos tinku exploatavimas" and heating pipe in the bathroom)	Gas AND LPG	No data
Monthly	Electricity, gas, LPG, wood, coal, liquid, other fuel, central	Gas AND LPG	No data
Two weeks	Electricity, LPG, heating oil, wood, coal, briquettes, central	Only LPG	Own prod wood

Survey	Type	Number of households in ECAPOV file	Households with no housing expenditure (%)	Households with no energy expenditure (zero) (%)	Share of housing in total expenditure (%)	Share of utility in total expenditure (%)	Share of energy in total expenditure (%)
Montenegro 2009	HBS	1223	1.1	1.4	13.97	11.77	10.45
Poland 2009	HBS	37302	2.5	6.6	17.03	17.02	12.95
Romania 2009	HBS	31598	2.7	3.0	14.87	14.47	12.27
Russian Federation 2008	HBS	51288 (Q1) 51296 (Q2) 51291 (Q3) 51300 (Q4)		4.85 (Q1) 4.92 (Q2) 5.24 (Q3) 4.43 (Q4)		12.18	7.01
Serbia 2009	HBS	4592	1.8	2.7	15.16	13.41	11.90
Tajikistan 2009	PANEL	1503	0.5	0.1	15.08	15.51	15.14
Turkey 2009	HBS	10039	3.3	7.3	13.73	11.68	9.82
Ukraine 2008	HBS	10622	0.4	0.3	7.31	7.25	6.32

Frequency of info on energy expenditure	Energy expenditures identified	Treatment of gas and LPG	Collected Wood
Quarterly	Electricity, LPG, solid, (wood+coal), liquid, central	Only LPG	firewood from own plot
Monthly	Electricity, gas, LPG, wood, coal, liquid, other fuel, central	Gas AND LPG	No data
Monthly	Electricity, gas, LPG, wood, coal, kerosene, heating oil, central	Gas AND LPG	No data
Monthly for utilities/quarterly for fuels	Electricity, gas, LPG, wood, coal, peat, other, liquid, central	Gas AND LPG	
Quarterly	Gas, LPG, wood, coal, w-central (includes hot water)	Gas and LPG	Own wood
Monthly for utilities/monthly for fuels for winter/summer	Electricity, LPG, wood, coal, diesel, liquid, central	Gas expenditures are missing	
Monthly	Electricity, gas, LPG, solid, liquid, w-central (means hot water steam and ice)	Gas AND LPG	
Quarterly/ annualized	Electricity, gas, LPG, solid, liquid, w-central (heating is combined with hot water)	Gas AND LPG	In questionnaire

This report is a part of a series of 3 regional reports. The series includes *Growing Green: The Economic Benefits of Climate Action, Balancing Act: Cutting Energy Subsidies While Protecting Affordability* and *Energy Efficiency: Lessons Learned from Success Stories*.

Growing Green: The Economic Benefits of Climate Action

Besides growth and social inclusion, the third strategic priority for the ECA Region is addressing the problem of climate change. Adaptation to a changing climate is already a concern in several ECA countries that have experienced severe droughts affecting crops and hydropower generation. A regional study on adapting to climate change and several national adaptation pilots have analyzed these issues. This report is a complementary study which explores options for reducing the region's greenhouse gas emissions. It focuses on the three main ways to do so: use less energy, use cleaner energy, and better manage natural systems that store vast amounts of carbon. The study discusses policy priorities across sectors — in power generation, production, mobility, the built environment and natural environment. Making climate sustainability a higher priority will involve trade-offs. A low carbon energy transition imposes costs on firms and households, but it also generates new economic activities. The study proposes strategies how countries can reduce harmful impacts from climate action policies and get the most out of emerging opportunities.

Energy Efficiency: Lessons Learned from Success Stories

The report is designed to identify energy efficiency policies that have been implemented in countries that have successfully decreased their energy intensity. The study analyzes the energy efficiency policies in seven successful EU countries: Denmark, Germany, Ireland, Sweden, Lithuania, Poland and Romania. These countries were achieved low energy intensities or reduced their energy intensity considerably over the past twenty years. The report analyzes the evolution of the energy intensity of these countries from 1990 to 2007, identifying points of inflection in the progress towards improvements. Changes to the policy agenda immediately upstream are explored in an effort to identify cause and affect relationships in energy use. The country case studies indicate that policy implementation evolves, reflecting such issues as institutional capacity and affordability. For example, energy price increases were adjusted quickly to reflect full economic costs for all sectors except households in EU-12 countries. EU-15 countries have added environmental taxes to energy costs, providing deeper incentives to constrain energy use. Implementing environmental taxes was difficult and generally took place when it appeared to be politically viable to do so. Similarly for governance issues, EU-12 countries have undertaken some of the first steps towards improving the governance of the energy efficiency agenda by establishing an entity responsible for energy efficiency policy and preparing National Energy Efficiency Action Plans. Monitoring and Evaluation of these programs is functioning to a limited extent in EU-12 countries while EU-15 countries take these responsibilities more seriously as they are better able to afford the costs associated with such programs.